Opening

Our Moral Eye

DREAM ANGEL. 1960?
High-fired ceramic. 10″ x 6″

Opening
Our Moral Eye

Essays, Talks, & Poems

Embracing Creativity & Community

M. C. RICHARDS

edited by Deborah J. Haynes

 Lindisfarne Press

Acknowledgment

Every work has a specific genealogy. A few years ago, M. C. told me that she wanted to see her 1980 essay, "The Public School and the Education of the Whole Person," in print once again, in order to respond to repeated requests for the piece. I offered to help her gain permission to reprint this essay; the concept of a volume of essays, poem, and paintings of the 1980s and 1990s was born in the following months, as I wrote letters and had conversations. Christopher Bamford, in particular, was enthusiastic about publishing a book of her recent work. Now that book is a reality. I especially thank him for his vision of this project. — *Deborah J. Haynes*

"Toward M.C." is an edited version of a conversation between M.C. Richards and Gerry Williams held in Kimberton, PA, and Boston, MA, in August, 1985, it appeared in *Studio Potter* 14 (no.1); "The Public School and the Education of the Whole Person" was originally published by The Pilgrim Press, New York, 1980; "After Wholeness" appeared in *Creation Spirituality*, November/December 1992, pp. 20-22; "The Renewal of Art through Agriculture" appeared in *Creation Spirituality*, March/April 1993, pp. 12-15. Many of the poems in the section "Before the Beginning: New Poems by M.C. Richards" have been printed in a book titled, *Before the Beginning*, published by Tangram, Berkeley, CA, 1995.

Published by Lindisfarne Press,
RR 4 Box 94-A1 Hudson, N.Y. 12534

This edition © 1996 by M. C. Richards

Library of Congress Cataloging-in-Publication Data
Richards, Mary Caroline.
    Opening our moral eye / M.C. Richards.
    ISBN 0-940262-78-9 (pbk.)
    1. Self-actualization (Psychology)   I. Title.
    BF637.S4R53 1996
    814'.54—dc20   96-41084

10 9 8 7 6 5 4 3 2 1

Contents

Author's Foreword   7

Homage by Deborah J. Haynes   13

M.C.'s Gift by Paulus Berensohn   17

M.C. and Haystack by Francis Merritt   17

Toward M. C. *(Conversations with M.C.)* 19

Black Mountain College: A Personal View of Creativity   61

The Public School and the Education of the Whole Person   77

After Wholeness, What?   113

Imagination and Authenticity as Doorways to Creation   118

The Renewal of Art through Agriculture   134

Creativity and the Practice of Awe   140

Before the Beginning: New Poems by M.C. Richards   145

Biographical Sketch by Deborah J. Haynes   189

Afterword by Deborah J. Haynes   193

My hunch is that morality is a strong sense of connection,
that it is built in, as are connections themselves,
and that the moral imagination may be awakened
as the sense of wholeness is awakened.

FROM THE AUTHOR'S FORWARD

Author's Foreword

My hunch is that morality is a strong sense of connection, that it is built in, as are connections themselves, and that the moral imagination may be awakened as the sense of wholeness is awakened. Our moral eye is the organ which understands connections between things, understands consequences, and attempts to maintain its commitment to the life of nature and humanity.

I had initially wanted to call this book *A Communion of Worlds*, inspired by what the angels are singing in my poem "Opening Song": "In art is a communion of worlds." For in this book are collected a series of pieces from the worlds of education, agriculture, moral philosophy, creation spirituality, poetry, social justice and social imagination, creativity, biography. One meaning of *art* can be gained by looking at its ancient Indo-European root, *ar*, which means to join. It is an old syllable that knits together as, for example, in *harmony*. It also connects with the world of numbers in *logarithm* and the world of religion in *ritual*.[1] Hence, "in art is a communion of worlds."

Art integrates also the verbal and non-verbal worlds, showing the work of the hands to be soul language, and the energies of

---

1. This etymology is taken from the section on Indo-European roots in *The American Heritage Dictionary* (p. 1506). *Ritual* comes from the Latin *ritus*, a variant suffixed form of *ar*.

speech to be translations of non-verbal impulses. The speech organ is as mysterious as the Muse.

I changed the title in order to move toward a more difficult and challenging task. The Communion of Worlds is more or less given. Our moral eye struggles to awaken.

This new direction was first articulated by Deborah Haynes, who has edited this book and written its introduction. She had come upon the image in *Centering* of art as a moral eye, opening and closing; and she was taken by it. Her primary concern is a moral re-imagining of the vocation of the artist, the artist's calling. What is it really? Endowed with such gifts, how should creativity be used to heal our communities? How can a moral eye be awakened?

I personalized the task by making it "our" moral eye. In this way my commitment to community and communion is also expressed.

I am very indebted to the enthusiasm and faithfulness of Deborah, who set this book in motion and has seen it into publication. She shares as well a "communion of worlds," as she moves in a postdisciplinary universe of art and religion with the complex resonances of these concerns. She is an artist and teacher and author and gardener and has been my friend for many years.

My own feeling about this collection is celebrative, in praise and gratitude for the connections that exist, what our awakened moral eye perceives. My hope is that this book will strengthen the connective tissue where it has begun to grow, and bring joy to our embrace.

. . . .

"The Public School and the Education of the Whole Person" was written in response to an invitation from the United Church Board of Homeland Ministries, which had resolved to bring out a series of booklets to create fruitful discussion on the subject of the public school. The public schools are in crisis. How can the crisis be understood? How can it be healed?

I was asked to write a piece that would be the philosophical ground for the series: a philosophy of the whole human being, as best we can understand and foster it. It was a subject I could approach only intuitively, relying on creative connections in my psyche ready to be drawn upon. I am reminded of a sentence from the introduction to *Centering*: "Mystery sucks at our breath like a wind tunnel. Invites us into it. Let us pray, and enter." Composing this piece on the public school and the education of the whole person was like that. I put my hands on the typewriter keys, prayed, and began, as I often do, with the meanings of the words we are using as our map: "person," "education," "wholeness." They lead us into questions which become our playing field. As we play, we dream. Images appear to guide us. We continue close to the bone, close to the sense of truth and life, finding our way to the schooling we long for. When I am finished with the piece, I write the two poems (anthem and hymn) that frame the essay. It seems to me a well-integrated piece, juicy and timely.

My favorite piece in this volume is "After Wholeness, What?" I could have made this the title of the whole collection. It is an extremely important piece in my own development. For, as I say in it, I have spent my adult life trying to love the enemy and dissolve barriers, even though I also use quotes like "I love the tiger but I don't put my head in her mouth." Likewise, I love the computer but I don't put my head under its control. In this piece I tell about my radicalization in a university setting where for the first time I felt OUTRAGE at computer control and alarm at the numbness of the senses on the part of my friends and colleagues.

Another reason I like this piece is that it expresses a quality of my temperament which has been both an advantage and a disadvantage: namely, the impulse to question. So there's all this wholeness everybody is selling these days. And then? After wholeness, what?

"Imagination and Authenticity as Doorways to Creation" was an ambitious talk I gave in Oakland, California, as part of a program speaking to our need for soul growth and visionary courage. It witnesses to an essential intuitive cognition in us which connects us to the cosmos and to our creative self. It is meant to disarm the destructive habit of self-belittling and the random violence threatening our creativity.

It was after a trip to West Australia and a walkabout with an aboriginal family that I returned to my agricultural community with a clearer understanding of why I call my course "The Renewal of Art Through Agriculture." I give this course to farm apprentices in our agricultural training program. Artistic activity, yes, but what does it have to do with agriculture?

"Creativity and the Practice of Awe" had a very special genesis which I describe in the piece. It came out of life situations in which awe was absent, and which were transformed by its rebirth. It then gives one answer to the question, "If you can't already experience awe, how do you generate it?"

"Black Mountain College: A Personal View of Creativity" is largely autobiographical. Black Mountain College (1933-1956) in the Smoky Mountains of North Carolina, was an important development in the history of education in this country. It has attracted as much, or more, interest since its adjournment as it did during its thirty-three years of life.

I went there to teach English in 1945, after leaving the University of Chicago in dissatisfaction with the materialistic competitive greed of the students I was trying to teach. I was drawn to Black Mountain by an interest in its program of studio arts, intellectual disciplines based on the imagination, community work program and self-government, simple living, freedom from grades, tenure, departments, accreditation . . . and attractive to scholars, artists, farmers, community builders—we were the first college in the South to have an interracial policy. In 1992, a reunion and educational conference was organized in

San Francisco by the DeYoung Museum education department. I was asked to speak about my experience.

"Toward M.C." is a take on the title of my book, *Toward Wholeness*. Gerry Williams, potter and teacher and editor of *Studio Potter*, came to our community for several days to talk with me and prepare a possible piece for his magazine, with photos. This is what it turned into, without the photographs. The "Dream Angel" described in the opening paragraph appears as the frontispiece of this volume.

The three eyes of the Dream Angel outstrip even the imagination of "our moral eye." They are wide open, and they integrate the warmth of the Sun, the essence of the Diamond, and the Human Self. They look with affectionate wisdom on our efforts to awaken. They know we are on our way. The angel smiles.

M. C. RICHARDS
Camphill Village, Kimberton Hills, PA
November 24, 1995

Homage

by Deborah J. Haynes

How do we honor those whom we love? How do we acknowledge, within a public sphere, that each of us is not the product of an isolated consciousness with solitary aspirations, but that we owe the fullness of our humanity—our sense of possibility and potential—to significant encounters with other persons? Individual intention, will, and labor are essential, but we need an Other to create the self. Like all persons, artists are not born; they are created through a myriad of such encounters. Then, the vessel that is formed as a result of these exhortations and encouragement from teachers and mentors, combined with the disciplines of artistic practice, is fired to produce a person, an artist.

I first met M. C. Richards at the University of Oregon in Eugene, in 1971. The ceramics studio at Oregon was deeply influenced by the production pottery ethos that defined the 1960s. In this context, where the emphasis was on our direct experience with the materials, a few texts were also called to our attention. David Green's *Understanding Pottery Glazes* and Daniel Rhodes' *Clay and Glazes for the Potter*, were consulted on technical questions. D'arcy Thompson's *Growth and Form*, Christopher Alexander's *Synthesis of Form*, Gaston Bachelard's *Psychoanalysis of Fire*, and Guy Murchie's *Music of the Spheres* were consulted for aesthetic and philosophical guidance.

But, in the winter of 1971, another book was urged on us: *Centering: in Pottery, Poetry, and the Person* by Mary Caroline Richards.

13

Originally published in 1964, the first paperback edition appeared in 1969. Our teachers read it with excitement and invited us to read it too. Here was a philosophy of creativity and a philosophy of life. If books such as Green's and Rhodes' might be said to provide the body of ceramics, Bachelard's and Murchie's the intellect, then *Centering* was an attempt to articulate its soul.

In her book, Richards talked in a poetic language about the connections between our work as potters who center clay—who create pots that must withstand the ordeal by fire—and about the hard work of becoming a self capable of responding, in life and in art, to other persons. Here, for the first time, I encountered a vision and articulation of the moral dimension of artistic work. "How do we do it," she wrote, "how do we center in the moral sphere? How do we love our enemies? How do we perform the CRAFT of life, *kraft*, *potentia*?" *Kraft* means power or strength; and we must use that power to form not just the pot, but ourselves. Art, Richards insisted, is a "Moral Eye" which opens and closes, helping us to see truly and to live into those questions. At the center of her vision is no product to sell, no "specific object" that artists such as Donald Judd touted in the 1960s, but a process of becoming, of evolution.

Richards' writing appealed to me because it was vivid, personal. This was no disembodied abstract philosophy. She told jokes, describing how we tear and swat and push and pinch and squeeze and caress and scratch and model and beat the clay. She related philosophical ideas to her life as a poet, a potter, a teacher, an "odd bird" in both academic and craft worlds. She talked of the paradox of longing for union and separation, and of the pain, suffering, and joy that accompany our attempts to live and love. At the center of all our yearning and urgent activity lie mystery and paradox.

M. C. is fond of reminding us that the root of the verb "to educate" is *educare*, to draw out or to body forth. With such an awkward phrase, she directs attention to the fact that we are incarnate souls. If indeed the authenticity of metaphor is the result of the intrinsic relationship of that metaphor to what is being described,

14

then this may explain the extraordinary appeal of M. C.'s writing. Her books are filled with metaphors drawn from poetry, from physical sensual life, and from the crafts. Language, for M. C., is alive. It breathes, has blood, a tongue, a body. "Language is alive in the center from which the poet draws. It has its bright blood and call still upon it. It has not become a symbol nor an abstraction nor a concept merely. It thrills in the breath like any tongue or banner. You cannot feel that life by thinking about it. You can feel it only by waking into it as into a dream.... To be a poet is to bring some of the sleep into the waking. To be a whole person is to let the poet live in oneself and to center the dreaming and the waking."

But her metaphors don't just apply to verbal language, to poetry. Centering the clay on the potter's wheel and then using it to make a shape, she says, is analogous to hearing and making a poem. "To bring universe into personal wholeness, to breathe in, to drink deep, to receive, to understand, to yield, to *read* life. AND to spend wholeness in act, to breathe out, to give, to mean, to say, to *write*, to *create* life." With the word, as with the clay, we read life and write life: we create life. We live through the word, the word lives through us. We breathe into the clay, the clay lives.

I had recognized M. C.'s voice in *Centering* as a distinctly female voice. Yes, it was written in the prose of the early 1960s when "he" referred to a man or woman, when "man" or "mankind" meant all human beings. Yet her voice was personal: she wove philosophical reflection with stories and personal anecdote, speaking about her fear and longing, her seemingly contradictory yearning for union and separation. About love and death. Both the form and the content of her prose touched me deeply. "It takes courage," she had written, "to grow up and turn out to be who we are. We face surprises. And disappointments. The crucial fact is that we are different from anybody we know or admire.... It takes all one's courage to be the person one is, fulfilling one's odd and unique possibilities...."

M. C. was my first female teacher in the arts, and she articulated what I saw in the 1970s as a distinctively feminine perspective when she talked about clay, art, and life. Although I resist such essentialist stereotypes now, I cannot simply dismiss my earlier perception and response. I responded to M. C. as a teacher and as a woman; my reaction was linked to attempts to understand and express my own female identity.

A hint that this might be more broadly relevant in assessing M. C.'s work as an artist and teacher was suggested to me by Mary Phillips in a conversation in Berkeley, California, in 1994. M. C.'s work, Mary said, was especially important for women, although no one had yet really articulated this publicly. As far as I know, M. C. has not linked her personal development, educational work, or spiritual search to women's struggles for identity and equity in the second half of the twentieth century. Nevertheless, her influence on my life, and on the lives of many others, can be interpreted in these terms. What does it mean to be a woman? To be a woman and an artist? To be a woman and a teacher? How are the longings of love related to aspirations concerning work?

Sigmund Freud claimed that love and work form the foundation of civilization and communal life. Eros, he said, provides the impetus that drives Ananke, the external necessities that govern what we do in order to live. Reflecting patriarchal social structures, Freud insisted that the most fateful questions for the human species—and in light of recent environmental awareness, for all living beings and the earth itself—concern the extent to which civilization and its institutions can control human aggression and destruction.

While M. C.'s life and work demonstrate the veracity of Freud's insight into the formative significance of love and work, her life and work also function as a foil to Freud's gendered reflections. M. C. has always been concerned with the development of spirit, and soul, through life and art. She has negotiated the boundaries between love and work, as a woman. The way she has articulated that process in words, pots, and paintings has been meaningful to me, and, I suspect, to many other women and men who are searching for models of integrated living, working, and acting in the world.

16

M.C.'s Gift

by Paulus Berensohn

For as long as I have known her, M.C. has had a deep feeling and concern for community and the role of artistic behavior in it. It has been a lifelong personal longing which she is now living out at the Camphill Village for the Mentally Handicapped. She is practicing what she preaches, not out of some great ambition but in small daily increments.

Her gift to us lies in the way she lays images on us. Her scholarship and imagination become visual seed images which open us up to new connections and insights. She keeps reminding us, fruitfully, that it is not just pots we are making but our whole life that we are forming.

M.C. and Haystack

by Francis Merritt

M.C. Richards has done so much over the last twenty-five years to define the Haystack ideal in her direct association and influence, both as a teacher and trustee, and to symbolize it in her own life and work as a poet-potter, that any assessment of the relationship can only score it as a fortuitous historical and evolutionary flowering for Haystack. All of this becomes compounded treasure for me as it lives in the objective reminder, which is her pottery in my collection, and which I am emboldened to appraise as some of the most distinguished American ceramics of my generation.

Toward M.C.

This article is an edited version of conversations taped in 1985 with Gerry Williams, editor of Studio Potter, *who gave it this title.*

Once in a dream I was standing in my vegetable garden. Fifty feet away, on the compost pile, stood a Being smiling strangely. It had three eyes. The right eye was a sun, the middle eye was a diamond, and the left was a human eye but huge, as large as the diamond and sun. This Being had a benign expression on its countenance. Its front teeth were crooked in a way mine used to be.

In my dream I found myself asking the Being a question, a kind of life or destiny question, the kind of question one might ask the I Ching book of oracles. The question began: "When will I ... when will my time ... what is my destiny?" I can hardly find words now to describe the question in my dream. It was a question in a question, a wide kind of question that, looking back on it, one feels a compassion for oneself at that moment in the search for truth when one asks the divine realm for feedback.

The Being, who seemed to be from the daimonic realm, answered, "I wouldn't worry about that if I were you."[1]

The dream had such an impact on me that when I awoke I went straightaway to the studio to fashion the head of the Being out of clay. I crumpled up newspaper and fit slabs of clay around it—the only way I knew to make a head at that time. I used a flameware clay which fired to an almost white color. This head has always

---

1. *Daimonic* is a divine power; *demonic* is an evil spirit.

had a special place among my things, though some people are not always comfortable with it.

I have had several powerful dreams and image experiences, though they have not been frequent. Actually that part of life was released into my consciousness when I began to work with a Jungian psychologist whose practice it was to introduce one's own unconscious through the medium of dreams. I would write down my dreams and talk about them in the sessions. The process encouraged a weaving back and forth between the dream mind and waking mind and was very fruitful.

Many of the ceremonial pots and images I make might be said to be primarily intuitive in their source, certainly in the source of their form. Making the I Am plaques, for example, might be called an intuitive act, as it is with things I make out of a sense of ritual or seasonal festival.

I believe intuition is, however, a form of cognition. You do not leave cognition for something else, but you move more and more confidently between the life of intuition and that of daily consciousness. My interest in cognition has really been an interest in truth: "What's going on here?" It's a matter of becoming perceptive at the sensory level as well as at the intuitive level about processes going on in the natural world or in another human being or in oneself. These are not two separate realms, though they may have seemed so at one time because a certain kind of knowledge is encouraged in one's schooling where intuitive cognition is thought to be the luxury of the poet. Now I know that it is the artistic mind which is the whole mind.

There is an old saying that life itself is the biggest art. I've felt that all the so-called arts are an apprenticeship preparation for behavior and relationship which is more inclusive, a wider orbit. I don't know who was ever the first to refer to the wholeness of our life and of the cosmic reality as being art. The clue is given in the word *art* itself. When we trace it to its origins as best we can, we find an old Indo-European syllable, *ar*, which meant "to fit together, to join." An example would be in the word *harmony* from the Greek word *harmos*, which means "shoulder where two bones are fitted together." The idea of art being the practice of finding connections, of fitting things together is very open ended. Where does the connecting stop?

The same syllable is to be found in the root of *arithmetic, logarithm*, and *ritual*. These are all practices of connecting—all interconnected at the root, a wholeness made of diverse elements. The word *order* is interesting here. It comes from the art of weaving and originally meant the arrangement of threads on a loom. But isn't weaving a practice of interconnecting threads going in opposite directions: up and down and back and forth? To think of order and harmony and art in this way—as a fusion of opposites—tends to heal the divisions we might be tempted to make. Images! Imagination! Peace through paradox! Somewhere deep in the past of our archaic souls, artistic mind prepared its long journey to consciousness. It kept to the mystery at the core (*coeur?*) and yet learned to behave in cultural history. The gods have sacrificed much in their love of humankind. So much of their own spontaneity and inspired craziness. Maybe this inspired diversity is what it actually means to say life is an art. What else could it possibly be!

> > > > >

I was born in Weiser, Idaho, which is on the Snake River on the border with Oregon, a little town with wheat and sheep. I did very little more than get born there. I was brought up in Portland, Oregon. My father did a number of things. He had gone to law school in Indiana and had come west with his wife and first child, my sister, to do some kind of homesteading. But when he got to Weiser, he found that promise didn't exist. He became a young prosecuting attorney for the county, which was the wrong thing for him to be because he was not a political man at all. As I understood it from his telling me, he was not really successful.

When the war came, he moved with his family to Portland where he built ships and never went back to law. He became a salesman for Wearever Aluminum, where he learned to make wonderful pancakes and cornbread to demonstrate the ware. And most importantly, he was a salesman for *Compton's Pictured Encyclopedia* for schools and libraries. He traveled around Oregon selling these encyclopedias. He liked doing it and admired the teachers in the country schools. His dearest wish for me was that I should be an elementary school teacher in that tradition. The influence of my father was very palpable. He was an earnest man, and I was his favorite child. And so he would let himself be a little more expressive. He used to play baseball and football with me out in the street. When I got older I was struck by how, when I asked him a question, he would often say "I'll have to think about that." And maybe two or three days afterward he would say, "I've been thinking of what you asked me, and this is what I think about it...." I thought that was terrific. He gave it his full attention. And said what he had to say.

My maternal grandfather was said to be a rascal who spent all his time telling stories at the country store instead of taking care of his motherless children, whom he gave away on the birth of the ninth child and the death of his wife. My mother, Lily Kate Ulen, was nine years old at the time. She would tell me the story over and over again of how she and her two sisters, Mary and Anna, walked down the road together to find someone to live with. My mother went to a few different places before she found a home with a Quaker couple who had a little girl about her age. My mother was a good worker and bright and loving (or so I pictured her). How deeply awed I was by this scene of courageous little girls setting out hand-in-hand to find their lives.

My paternal grandfather is a story too. Suffice it to say that after a saloon brawl which nearly finished him off with abdominal stab wounds, he (David Riley Richards) promised to preach God's mercy and forgiveness if he could be allowed to recover. In due course he became a field preacher of the Dunkard Church of the Brethren. It was a deal. He preached, had thirteen children (two wives), and excommunicated his son Jesse Linley for entering such a worldly profession as the law. Just to round this off... I was named Mary Caroline after my two grandmothers, Mary Clementine and Emily Caroline. Just think, I might have turned up as Emily Clementine!

My mother and I took a trip East when I was twelve. We stopped in Wyoming to visit Uncle Ernest and his two daughters about my age. One evening I got up on top of one of the farm outbuildings. I was seen walking the ridgepole. My cousins became alarmed and ran into the house to ask what could be done. My mother came out and saw me up there on the ridgepole and said, "Oh, Mary Caroline, your silhouette is so beautiful against the sunset." Well, maybe that indicates the space for poetry. My mother was the kind of person who cut out poems from the newspaper and put them up around the kitchen. She remembered lines from her high school production of *Hamlet* and could say a lot of them. I had a brother who was gifted musically. It was clear his gift and artistry was enormously respected and admired by everyone. One got the message that artistic gift was valued and respected.

> > > > >

I loved going to school. First I went to junior college in Portland, St. Helen's Hall Junior College. There I wrote the words of the school anthem, edited the *Scintilla*, our yearbook, and made the fencing and basketball teams.

Then I got a scholarship to Reed College. I majored in literature and languages. I had an English teacher in junior college who thought highly of me and gave me a book, a present after I finished her course, of an anthology of translated Oriental verse, edited by Eunice Tietjins. I was enthralled. So I began to wish to be a translator of Oriental poetry. Arthur Waley was my ideal. I went to Reed College with that in mind, to be a sinologist. I wanted to devote my life to making accessible in English those wonderful poems in classical Chinese. There was no Oriental Studies Department at Reed, but still I was allowed to do my bachelor's thesis on the topic of "Poetry of the T'ang Dynasty in Relation to Western Imagism."

I went to the University of California at Berkeley for graduate school, partly because I had a brother in Oakland right next door who managed a local theater and, if I got myself into straits, he would be family nearby.

I enrolled in the Oriental Studies Department hoping to develop a vocabulary quickly so that I might begin my work. The beginning Chinese course was taught by two men, one Oriental and the other Austrian. Ferdinand Lessing later became greatly honored as the maker of the Sanskrit-Chinese dictionary. He taught us, not vocabulary, but the morphology of the ideogram, the order of the brush strokes, the rising or falling tones. It was a privilege to be the student of such an uncommon scholar. But alas, it was not geared to my needs. At the rate we were going, it would be years before I could read even a newspaper.

I had a terrible decision to make: should I quit graduate school, go to San Francisco, and hire a tutor in Chinatown? Or should I sacrifice that and return to an English major? I was making my living by waitressing. It didn't seem realistic. With great anguish, I decided not to go on and began again my concentration on languages and literature, this time in English.

It's interesting, isn't it, that my attraction toward the East was to the language. That language in the East is all calligraphy and drawing; it's really a culture in which writing is drawing. So, the conception of writing as a handcraft I have had no problem with at all.

Later, in preparing the book on Rudolf Steiner education, I came across his discussions with teachers in which he traces the development of language from the sculptural and the musical. Handwriting still keeps some sculptural sense. And eurythmy, a movement-art of visible speech originated by Steiner, creates sculptural-musical forms which are the counterparts of words. It's not how the word "looks," but how its appearance comes about, as in the Chinese. My musings upon "writing as a hand-craft" are less visual in intent, more like a wholeness that inscribes itself in air (breath), swelling and slacking, curving and straight-ening. The mechanization of writing is a soul-threat. Keeping the word alive, words alive, speaking in our human voices—it makes a difference.

> > > > >

I did my doctoral dissertation on the theme of irony in Thomas Hardy. That too was interesting. Both writing-as-drawing and irony are interesting forerunners of what came later to be my jour-ney through Zen and the Anthroposophy of Rudolf Steiner. Irony occurs when there is a difference between appearance and reality, when you say one thing and mean another. In dramatic irony in a play where you have a case of mistaken identity, you appear to be following a realistic theme while all the time it's getting you into difficulty. How do we experience appearance and reality? Both have functions. An interesting thing about Thomas Hardy within this general life of mine, this life journey, was reading this long sort of epic he wrote called *The Dynasts*. What's relevant here about the piece is that Hardy had a lot of choruses of spirits—the Spirit of the Furies, the Spirits of Time—as real drama, cosmic drama. I was struck by it. I just took it as being what it was, but later when I got to reading Rudolf Steiner's work about the Time Spirits—the Spirits of Form and of Movement, in other words, "the spiritual world"—where other people might stumble over that kind of language, the language itself didn't produce any ten-sion in me. When I would read a Western philosopher like Steiner who talks about Time Spirits, it seems plausible I would be drawn to that strain of reality.

> > > > >

I finished my doctorate at Berkeley in 1942 and started teaching in the English Department. There came a vacancy at a state college in Washington which had lost its whole English faculty to the defense industry. I decided to take a position there and I went up to Ellensburg. I took my bicycle, lived in a hotel, and ate in the Chinese restaurant across the street. Then I looked around the campus to see what there was to do. Their workshops were quite well equipped, as often happens in state teachers colleges. They had workshops in raising copper, woodwork, photography, and clay. I went into the clay room. I've been asked what there was in clay that attracted me. I think at that moment when I did clay for the first time I saw that there was nothing intervening between me and it. I didn't have to have any other knowledge, didn't have to have any previous experience or know about tools or anything, just my hand and the clay—that was a powerful experience. Some might think it was laziness that I didn't get involved in something in which I had to master a process before I could do anything. But in this clay studio there was no wheel. I hadn't even heard of the potter's wheel. There were molds that you poured, and then this magical thing happened—you know, the plaster mold drinks in the water until you have a little wall, and then you pour out the clay. Pretty soon you have a vase to give to your sister or whatever. Then there was coil building. The first thing I ever made was a lapel pin that you pat out and cut. It was a black sheep. I made that and pasted the pin on the back. I also made some tiles which I decorated. The whole experience was just transporting, I must say. That was my first experience with the clay. I remember being wowed by the sensation. It was like a door opening, you know. Not verbal at all, and yet it was so tangible, so expressive. That was the first experience I had of the nonverbal clay, nonverbal thinking. I left Ellensburg at the end of that year and went on with my life in Santa Fe.

> > > > >

I was married in Santa Fe and worked on the newspaper. I also drove a taxi for the I Am Taxi Company. Then got divorced, went on to Chicago. I left that part of the world to go on about my business, which was, in a certain sense, to go on toward Black Mountain College. I put it this way because I had met a man in my senior year at Reed, John Kelley, who had been a student at Black Mountain. He had told me about it and showed me a brochure. The pictures in the brochure showed a table with students and faculty sitting around in work clothes, informal attitudes of conversation, and the environment was a working construction site. I was enormously taken with it. When my life in Santa Fe didn't work out, the only thing I knew to do in the future was to go see Black Mountain.

On the way I stopped at the University of Chicago. I had a friend there, teaching English. The assistant dean took me to lunch and, before I knew it, he had offered me a job teaching at the University. I accepted but soon discovered it was not going to be the place for me. Even though I felt honored to be hired at such a prestigious school, it turned out that whatever prestige it has wasn't in my line. The intellectuality of the place was one-sided and burdensome. In the spring I wrote Black Mountain about coming down should they have an opening. They wrote back and sent a student application form; they thought I was applying as a student! We finally got our correspondence cleared up and, yes, suddenly there was a faculty opening.

I went down there in the summer to be interviewed and to give a talk. The talk was on "Irony in Joseph Conrad." They offered me the position. Then back to Chicago, where I was having a love affair with a professor of sociology and logic, named Albert William Levi, Jr. I couldn't see how I could go off to Black Mountain just like that, without any emotional support. So I told them if they wanted me to come, they would have to take him too. He passed the interview partly because he talked about Whitehead, which was right up Annie Albers' creek.

In September, Bill and I hurried to the Justice of the Peace and got married. When we got to Black Mountain (that would be in the summer of 1945), there were only about fifty students there. There had been one of those characteristic schisms shortly before, and a passel of faculty had left and taken some of the students with them. The issue had to do with the speed at which the college should develop its interracial policy. The college was set in a rural environment in North Carolina, east of Asheville about fifteen miles, in a beautiful cove containing Lake Eden, with buildings like an old country inn. There was a Bauhaus connection because the Alberses, Josef and Annie, had been at the Bauhaus. They were very powerful at Black Mountain at that time. Though they didn't formally run the school because it was run by a board of fellows, in my husband's opinion they ran it.

I went there to teach English—reading and writing. I found an old printing press there on the property, and I and my students sorted out the type and cleaned it up. We started the Black Mountain Press, which was a wonderful experience. I printed my first volume of poems on that press in 1947 and bound the volumes, an edition of fifty. It's a great discipline actually, to set the type for what you've written; you have a different kind of scrutiny of the comma and the semi-colon and the capital letter, the indentation, and all of that—all of the expressive furniture of the written language.

There was no clay work at Black Mountain. The artistic work tended to be painting and drawing, drama, music, and some sculpture. There was no interest in clay while Josef Albers was there. He had a low opinion of clay as a medium for serious work.

He thought of it as a kind of ashtray art. After he left, we were in touch with Robert Turner. Turner was invited to come, he brought his kiln builder with him, and they built a kiln and a pottery studio with three or four wheels. He was my first teacher.

Bob Turner was new at teaching. He gave us one of our first problems: to design a tumbler, make a plaster form for casting, cast six or eight, and then decorate them. He taught me to throw on the potter's wheel. It was from him that I had the first image of the clay breathing, opening and taking in the air. The other extraordinary thing about his teaching was that he's the only potter whom I've ever seen at work who would come back to a pot the next day after it was thrown and throw on it some more. Bob would throw on a plaster bat, take the bat off the wheel, put it with the pot in the damp box, come back the next day and continue to throw it until it was just right. A contrast to much of the advice one gets, which is: don't overwork the clay. I really appreciated his freedom from the stereotypes.

I was making little casseroles. I was interested even then in cooking pots. We had lived the whole winter of 1949 in the south of France. I liked the French folk pottery so much that I even asked one place if they would take me on. I thought I wouldn't go back home: "I'll stay here and become a potter." Of course they thought I was daft, this American lady. The shop was a family affair and, if anyone was going to come on as a potter, it was going to be their fourteen-year-old or their nephew. So when I worked at Black Mountain, I wanted to make things like French cooking ware. I made a body, half red burning clay and half fireclay, and made little casseroles, and I used them with direct fire. I think David Tudor probably still has two or three pieces of mine from that era.

I studied one summer with Warren MacKenzie for three weeks, Daniel Rhodes for three weeks, and Peter Voulkos for three weeks. Somebody at Black Mountain invited them, so somebody was on the ball. They also got the Hamada-Leach-Yanagi trio to come down, but I was not there for that.

MacKenzie came first. He came with a wonderful knapsack of examples of thrown stoneware. I'd never seen anything like them. One cup and saucer by Lucie Rie broke my heart, they were so beautiful. There is a passage in *The Crossing Point* about it, where I talk about going to London to pay her homage and also to get a cup and saucer like that. She wouldn't sell me one but she gave me one. And in exchange I made her a poem. It's in the last talk, called "Work and Source, Concerts of Space (for Lucie Rie)." It was a terrific turn-on, MacKenzie showing those things. He also had a lively, rhythmic way of working and teaching. He was one of those people who says you should make 500 mugs before you keep one. And I thought, "you're kidding... I'll keep everything." Even if the things weren't quite on center, it didn't bother me that much.

Dan Rhodes concentrated on throwing, although he did make some assignments like doing some texturing and putting on handles where the handles should go. Right away I realized that there was often going to be a kind of conflict between the aesthetic assumptions of those who knew and my own joy, whatever it was, in the putting on of the handle. Like: "Oh no, it mustn't go there, it must go here..." or "It mustn't go on the rim because the rim will go out of shape." I didn't know what the rim would do. But I took it all in. I never did learn how to put on a handle and then pull it, which I would have liked to do. Dan was a good teacher, and he was also generous with glaze formulas. He gave me lots of formulas for cone 04.

Peter Voulkos was doing his big vase forms, doing them, as he said, to have a surface to decorate, to play with. We got experience with sgraffito and resist. Peter was important in my life for a couple of reasons—things he said became like meditations in my soul. One of them was: Work with it until it collapses. The other was: There is plenty more where this came from. That feeling of making things in order to have surfaces to play on: I like that, I do that. I start out to make a series of things like a set of mugs. But before I know it, one is not like the other, even in the glazing. Play in this context would be diverging from a pattern, and play would somehow win out. I don't deliberately say I'll make them different, I just do it. Then I ask myself: "Why did I do that? Why can't I make them all alike?" It could be that I'm just a poor thrower. But I can make them alike if I weigh the clay first and make things to measurement. I do enjoy the fooling around with clay and the glazing.

David Tudor was a musician, and we were at Black Mountain together after Bill Levi and I had separated. David at that time was John Cage's pianist. He was premiering the "Music of Changes." And he was also accompanist of Katherine Litz, the dancer. When Katherine came to Black Mountain, she brought David there to play, and John and Merce Cunningham came, and David played for them. He was an exceptional pianist. The picture of him I have in my memory is David performing on the grand piano in the dining hall, the lights shining on him for the performance. And I am standing over by the coffee urn with Lou Harrison, who was a composer there. I'm asking Lou, "Who is that?" David was playing five pieces by Alban Berg. Fantastic. And I'm saying dumb things like, "I thought he was Litz's accompanist...." David was a first-class musician. And generous in performing student work from Black Mountain composers. There's a little bit about this at the end of the first chapter of *Centering*, David Tudor performing one of these compositions—entering from the wings, performing, bowing, exiting, coming on again—all in total seriousness, professional. A striking thing to behold.

John Cage and I have been friends since the first time we met, which was in 1947 or '48, when John and Merce came to Black Mountain to give performances of dance and music. I had written some poetry, and John insisted on seeing it, which was nice. He liked it and said my work connected with two of the nine classic emotions from Indian esoteric something-or-other-Wonder and Mirth. I've never forgotten this. I was lucky and honored to be taken into friendship with them. They came back to Black Mountain for summer sessions, and Merce began his dance company there. It gave him a place to come for the summer and bring his gang. We fed them and they had a place to perform. Both John and Merce are still living, thank God;[1] there will be a big hole in the Earth when they go.

Black Mountain had a threefold program: community life, studio arts, and intellectual disciplines. Nobody could graduate from Black Mountain who didn't qualify in all three. That, in a way, was a threefold sketch of something that later on became a Threefold Image of the human being, which Rudolf Steiner talks about. It is a basic truth. I don't think of truth as being exclusive. I think of truth as entering by many doors, being inclusive. My book *Centering* is about bringing in, not leaving out. Some people think it's about some kind of inner stillness, the inner stillness before the creative act. I read something like that about *Centering* and I thought, "Oh, that sounds good, but that isn't what my book is about." They take the word *centering* and think they know what it means without bothering to find out how it's used. Anyway, if you want to live with all your burners lit, you live through this: community, self, and the artistic making. The community is like the relating self. The arts can be the creating self, and the pondering is the inquiring of the intellectual disciplines. We ask questions, try to find out why a plant grows up and not down. And why do we think the sun will come up tomorrow? That was one of the questions we put on the exam at Black Mountain.

Black Mountain was like a dream come true, a place where one could really be oneself with the mysteries of the individual and of communion between individuals, intact and at the edges of history, edges of inquiry, both open and rooted. That's why I took it so hard when it didn't work out. It wasn't just pride. My question had become: "If we can't do it here, where in the world can we do

---

1. John Cage died in 1993.

it?" At Black Mountain, we had nothing in our way but poverty, which is not important. We didn't have money, but we had total freedom to do all we wanted. If we couldn't get on with it there, where in the world could we do it? If we were so creative and imaginative, artistic, idealistic, and well educated, why was everything such a mess? But all this education and artistic hoopla at Black Mountain didn't keep anybody from knocking his neighbor down. Like Bill Levi and the militant Quakers in the hall of the study building, poking each other in the nose. Black Mountain did what it had to do and then adjourned. That's the way we put it in the record: it adjourned.

> > > > >

In my life there seems to be a thread of continuity, a journeying connecting earlier and later stages of my experience. An early interest in Oriental studies changed later to working with the Oriental tradition in clay and with Western traditions in writing as drawing. My being in Camphill now has such an emergent flavor about it, as if seeds were sown and then ripen into certain kinds of incidents or synchronicities.

Take theater, for example. When I was in junior college in Portland, I was active in the theater, first with the directors of the Portland Civic Theatre, Mary and Fred Harris. In Berkeley while I was in graduate school, I did some workshops with the Harrises and had a kind of feeling of destiny about theater. It turned out, though, that the imaginative experience of theater was overwhelming to my immature ego. My ego couldn't withstand the imaginative experience of roles other than myself and then come back to that self with full naturalness without a good deal of risk and suffering. So I put the theater on the back burner until I got to Black Mountain. The nature of the place, its tradition of theater, and its atmosphere quickened those seeds back to life. There I translated a couple of plays of Jean Cocteau, one called *Marriage on the Eiffel Tower*, and the other, *Knights of the Round Table*. I cast and directed *Marriage on the Eiffel Tower*, and it was performed in the dining hall at Black Mountain at Thanksgiving time. It was a wonderful realization, with an original score and an orchestra, the whole dining room transformed into one of the levels of the Eiffel Tower.

I also directed a Yeats play called *The Death of Cuchulain*. In that production we had an original score by painter-faculty Joe Fiore and choreography designed for performance on gravel! I had taken as the set the area under the studies building, graveled, as it had an outdoor staircase coming down from the floor above. The whole area was built up above the surrounding thickets. There were lots of possibilities for dramatic entrances and exits. I seemed to have a natural affinity for theater although I had no formal training in it. In clay workshops I have sometimes worked with themes of Stage and Personae, objects in a certain space, forms with a certain emotional relationship between them. For example, I have assigned the piece "Wrestling with the Daimonic" from *The Crossing Point*, and, concentrating on the final dream, have asked people to quickly list their fears, then to pick one to express in clay. Then I ask them to make a second form in relation to the first, namely, "the friend" who is there for us even if the fire is too hot and we have to run away. Fear and Friend, positioned in something like a stage space, spatially relating to each other.

When I went to New York with David Tudor, he gave me a book by Jean Louis Barrault, a French actor whom I admired. In his book, *Reflections on the Theater*, there is a chapter on Antonin Artaud, someone of whom I had never heard before. Barrault said in his book that, if he were going to give a course in dramatic criticism, he would find it essential to include Aristotle's *Poetics*, Horace, Cornell's "Preface to *Le Cid*," Craig's *On the Theater*, and Artaud's *The Theater and Its Double*.

I was aghast and fascinated too because I had taught dramatic criticism and had never heard of Artaud. I said this to David, and he asked if I would like to see a copy of Artaud's book. He went into the back room of this railroad apartment we were living in and came out with a typed manuscript of *The Theater and Its Double*. It was in French, and David apologized because he hadn't put in all the accent marks. You see, an occurrence like this is another bit of evidence of the interlinking of basic elements, as if life contains an artistic archetype, a paradigm which joins and connects people and events in this wonderful way.

I asked David where he had gotten this manuscript. He said a dancer lent it to him when he was about to premiere the Second Piano Sonata by Pierre Boulez for the International Contemporary Music Society in New York. He was having trouble with the piece, not with playing the notes (his abilities were prodigious) but in playing *the music*. So he began a correspondence with Boulez, asking the composer what he was thinking about when he composed that sonata. Boulez replied that he was thinking about Mallarme, the poet, about his poem "Le Coup de Dès," and about Artaud. So David procured a copy of the book on loan (no slim feat in itself) and made a typed copy of the whole thing. And that's how he happened to have that manuscript.

It was difficult French to read. I decided I would translate it sentence by sentence. That way I could offer it to my friends at Black Mountain, Charles Olson and Wes Huss, both of whom were involved in theater and could not read French. I knew they would be fascinated by this improbable work. That's how I happened to translate a work which hardly anyone had heard of at the time, which I couldn't get into a theater magazine. They wouldn't publish even a chapter of it because they found it exaggerated and "sophomoric." I believe that was their phrase. It was finally published in 1958 by Grove Press, just in time for the Living Theater, when it was presided over by Judith Melina and Julian Beck, permeated by the spirit of the Theater of the Absurd and the Theater of Cruelty, as Artaud called it. This phrase, Theater of Cruelty, when translated into English immediately became a can of worms. If you don't have any idea what it means, you can make up all kinds of things involving a lot of bloody stumps. Actually it's a term which has to do with the old mystery theater, of the Eleusinian theater, sacred theater, theater that can't be faked, where the absolutely necessary laws of existence prevail, which Artaud thought was far more important to develop than the psychological, verbal theater of the West. He was much taken by the ritual theater of Bali. Gradually Artaud's work became better known in America. He was credited with a certain energy which seemed to accompany a kind of shift that was taking place in the theater. Its central intent was repositioned, no longer in the psychological arena of, as Artaud says, "Who kisses better," the psychological, verbal arena, but rather in the arena of elements which turn the human being toward transformation, especially toward social transformation. Artaud felt that war and dope, violence and injustice of all kinds, were substitutes which people resorted to because of the impoverishment of life as a whole and the impoverishment of the arts. In theater, it doesn't have to happen. Hamlet isn't really killed on the set, he's virtually killed, and this is what Artaud called "virtual efficacy." An apparent deed carries the essence of the theatrical act, but not the physical, literal acting out. This Artaud called the "alchemical theater," and it is the source for the title of his book, *The Theater and Its Double*. It is a reference to alchemical theatre, one of social transformation, where events move materials, as in alchemy, into new conjunctions, as the alchemists of old used lead or red earth or dung as a starting point for transformation. The thinking is not literal but uses symbols for primary materials, and these materials undergo changes according to the arts of the alchemists. So Artaud's purpose, in my opinion, was important social renewal. And the book I translated was a little offering in that direction.

> > > > >

After I left Black Mountain, I went to New York and lived there about three years. I participated in the artists' club there, and in the circle of friends and artists around John Cage, Merce Cunningham, Morton Feldman, Christian Wolfe, Boulez, and David Tudor. I also spent a year reading aloud *Finnegan's Wake* with a couple of friends uptown. At the same time I was continuing my pottery work at Greenwich House, where I was given a studio apprenticeship in exchange for mixing glazes. In about 1954 or '55, a bunch of us who had been at Black Mountain were somehow impelled to think of another place where we could get together in a kind of community. With the financial help of Paul Williams, we got a 110-acre place at Stony Point, about thirty miles north of the George Washington Bridge, in Rockland County. It was supposed to go rather light on the community aspect except in the physical, materialistic way. We shared the land and expenses. We'd all gotten burned at Black Mountain and weren't ready to commit ourselves to a community, which can be devastating if that commitment is not effective or honored. For me, personally, the idea of community was very much alive in my heart. We built a pottery studio there, Karen Karnes, David Weinrib and I. We fired our great oil-burning kiln for the first time in 1955.

By this time, I was stumbling over the question, "What do I do?" It has taken me a while to call myself anything—a potter, an artist. The tentacles of the academic world are tight around one's psyche, that early conditioning which divides the world into intellectuals and artists, women and men, verbal and nonverbal. I didn't know if I was supposed to be a production potter or not. I had to earn my living. David and I were very poor. I was doing some modeling for an art class down the road for five dollars an hour, and I was also baby-sitting. In the pot shop, Karen was more knowledgeable about marketing; fortunately, when a buyer would come to look at her things, he would look at mine too. I started producing tea bowls and hanging planters that went right on the wall. I made some platters that I pressed on big stones I got out of the woods. But I discovered in a couple of years that I was not reliable; I couldn't be depended upon to continue a line. I wasn't efficient and didn't want to be efficient about the whole practice of marketing, advertising, keeping accounts, and all that. I didn't have the stomach for it. I would rather teach part-time at City College, which I did, in the English department. I made enough pots to pay my overhead, tried to make another thousand dollars for the year. I wanted to have the time and freedom in my own psyche to live in a way that felt close to my self and not separate, and to garden and do the things I liked within the Stony Point community.

Gradually I claimed to be a potter even though I was not a full-time potter. When Francis Merritt telephoned me from Haystack School, Maine, in 1961, he asked me to teach pottery at their new place on Deer Isle. They had just opened for their first session. "But," I said, "I'm a poet." He said, "I know who you are. Come teach pottery and bring your poetry." That was a big step he enabled me to make, to allow me to go there and be a potter who read her poetry to the community. I wasn't made to feel shallow or uncommitted because of it. It was through Francis Merritt also that I was invited to give the talk at Wesleyan University, which triggered the commission of *Centering*. The healing there of who I am and what do I do—am I a potter, am I a poet, am I a writer, am I a teacher, what am I, yes, yes, yes, I am this. Yes, Buddhist, yes Christian, yes Mohammedan, yes, sun worshipper, yes, all, why not, why not?

Haystack was important in the forming of my adult relationship to the crafts and to my own developing, original contribution to the craft culture. I am an odd bird. Several times I have taken flight from the Haystack Board, knowing that I am not a good board member, that I don't do the work. Jack Larsen wouldn't have it. He said he didn't have time for introspection and myth, so he was depending on me to keep that element alive.

38

At Penland in 1965 I conceived and directed a program, "Crossover: Toward a New View of Language, Verbal and Nonverbal." At Haystack I gave "Writing as a Handcraft." That pilot program, "Crossover," could really have been an important incision into the body of the craft movement if any notice had been taken. It just didn't occur to me for many years to take hold of it myself, to take the initiative and say "Now, what about this?" and get something going myself. I'd been slow to develop the abilities to do that, perhaps the emotional stability has taken me a while. We have to stop shouting from the back of the hall. We have to come up on stage and say whatever it is we have to say.

In the academic environment, there is just teaching English, reading and writing; there's no hands-on. Now, twenty years later after the impact of Rudolf Steiner's elementary education upon me, I have learned from children what writing is about. I refuse to let that belong solely to the children. Adults are the overlooked audience now. I think that's the difference between working in a university and working in Haystack and Penland. In the university, you have just a little bit of yourself going, however earnestly and intensely. I looked around and saw myself and my colleagues in terrible shape, alcoholic, despairing, competitive. And why? "Why?" I asked one of the Steiner education sages. I asked how is it that we, who are teaching these essential values, Plato and Milton, and god-knows-whom-else, how is it that these permanent values don't rub off on us? Why is the culture of the university so morally questionable? And he answered, "Because we underestimate the forces against us." We think that all we have to do is think a thought, say it's true, and everything else will follow. We don't take into account all the forces of attrition and hostility. We assume that, if we call a value true, its truth will immediately be recognized and hosannahs will be sung. This is a kind of conceit of the spirit, an idea I owe to Rudolf Steiner's work.

> > > > >

In 1964–65, I went through a personal crisis of considerable severity. I moved away from the Stony Point community and into New York City, where I enjoyed for three years a wonderful sixth-floor walk-up apartment, for which I paid $25 a month. It had a fireplace, a toilet, a kitchen, and a window-box where I grew my herbs and geraniums. Sundays I would go out scavenging for wood for my fireplace, just as though I were a country dweller. During that time I had come across the work of a woman named Olive Whicher. This Englishwoman had done a lot of work in plant growth and projective geometry. I had heard her speak and she interested me very much; her work seemed to be a mathematical counterpart to what I had been trying to discover. I decided to leave for England where she was going to be giving a course, to a little college in Sussex called Emerson College. I wrote Emerson and asked if I could take her course, and the answer was "no," but I kept asking. Finally, not only did I go and take the course, I stayed with Olive Whicher while I was there. This was an important experience in relation to another thread in my life, which has to do with Rudolf Steiner and his work, namely geometry and plant growth.

When I arrived in London, I was given a gift by the only person I knew in England, Molly Frances. It was a book called *Rose Garden and Labyrinth, a Study in Art Education,* by Seonaid Robertson. The book jacket said that Seonaid Robertson was a teacher at Goldsmiths College, University of London. I wrote her a fan letter. For a long time I didn't hear anything from her. When it was almost the hour for me to return to America from Paris, a letter came, much forwarded, from Seonaid Robertson saying that she had been in the United States and hoped very much that I would come and we would meet. I changed my plan, I flew back to London, and arranged to meet her at the station. While I was waiting to meet her, bouncing down the street came this English woman with a bunch of violets in her hand. We each came with a bouquet of violets for the other. Seonaid took me to lunch at the Refectory to meet the other faculty. There I met Charity James, who was founder and director of a curriculum laboratory at Goldsmiths College. Before the day was done I had been offered a job as visiting American professor for the following term. I said I couldn't possibly do it, that I had to go home because I had a date at Penn State Art Education Department to give a talk to the graduate students. Seonaid had just come from there, we were both stirring the pot at Penn State. Charity said, "Go there and come back." She gave me a plane ticket, and that's just what I did.

Seonaid Robertson is a real teacher, a teacher of art education. She lives her work, enriched by mythology and psychology; she has a strong Jungian orientation and is also strongly a follower of Herbert Read.

We found we were going in the same direction, my work confirmed in her work. It was like getting a new family. For the new age, you find new friends, new people who are working out of similar sources. With Charity James also, the same thing happened at the Curriculum Laboratory. Their whole pitch was about adult education, which they called Collaborative Learning, where the concept of the teacher as authority is no longer the binding alternative. There's too much now in the works that there are no authorities for. We're at the edge of new insights. We don't have any authorities in the same way.

I went to a kiln-building festival in Chichester in 1967 led by Ann Stannard. We built several kinds of kilns, woodburning, coke, pit, sawdust, oil drop—the whole thing. I was so stimulated by it that I invited Ann to America to have a kiln-building festival at Paulus' farm, which he had just gotten, north of Scranton about twenty-five miles, a hundred acres, house and barn and fields and lots of space to build kilns. I had first written home to ask Paulus and Karen Karnes if they wanted such a festival, if they thought we could bring it off. Nobody would get paid, everybody would have to share the cost of materials. They were enthusiastic.

We did it. I planted a garden early so that when the festival came in August there would be veggies to eat.

Paulus Berensohn came to Haystack in early 1961-62 and was in my workshop. Our friendship has been a strong one ever since. When I first met him at Haystack, he was only interested in throwing and perfecting his technique. I couldn't get him to handbuild, he just wouldn't mind his teacher! He was interested in fiber, in wrapping his pieces in yarn, which got to be trendy in due course. Paulus worked like a dancer, using all his body instead of just pirouetting on one toe.

After we did the kiln-building festival, I went back to my little walk-up on Spring Street in New York City. One soft October night, I was mugged, hurt, and robbed. Paulus said I should just leave that place, come up to his farm, and move out of that wretched city at once. So I moved up to the farm in 1968. Since that time, the farm has been divided into two fifty-acre parcels. One of those fifty acres belongs to neighbors who have built marvelous geodesic domes. They have a fire pond and raise cows and chickens, doing subsistence farming. We have the other parcel. Our big fields we rent to a nearby farmer who grows hay and silage corn. There's also a wooded area full of hickory, tulip, poplar, and maple, and lots of wild roses and apple trees. A wonderful location with southern exposure. You can sit on the front porch and see the east—and here's the dawn—and to the west—there's the sunset. It isn't a vacant sky.

Meanwhile, destiny has brought me here to Kimberton Hills, but I haven't moved away from the farm. My room there is intact, my books are there. I go back occasionally to see the beauty of the flowers that come in spring, those wonderful plantings of daffodils, tulips, iris, lilac, those lovely things.

At the farm I have a big studio made of cinderblocks and in great disarray at the moment. Most of the work I show and exhibit, my pots, are all in cartons there. (The pots have been moved to Kimberton Hills.)

> > > > >

After *Centering* was published in 1964 I never returned to steady employment but earned my living as a free-lance potter, poet, author, teacher. That means really the last twenty years I have lived in a kind of rhythmic alternation of leaving home to work here and there, in a variety of contexts (which appear in *The Crossing Point*) and returning to the farm to rest and recharge and to make pots and a garden. A lot of my work in the last few years has been by order. For these I make casseroles, mugs, pie plates, vases, dinner-ware—hopefully useful as well as soulful. Other things, like the "I Am's" from the Gospel of St. John, were made gratuitously, without any thought of where they might live. They were just made and found a life. I have made other ceremonial pieces. For example, when Kimberton Hills first started its agricultural program, I was asked to make the canisters which would hold the biodynamic preparations—camomile, oak bark, nettle, dandelion. These lid-ded and perforated jars are still in the wet, dark grotto where they were originally put to live. An even more ceremonial commission was made when Kimberton Hills asked me to make the Founda-tion Stones for its new community hall—Rose Hall, or the House of Dawn and Dusk. These hollow "stones" were two forms sug-gested by the community: one, a sun piece, like a bread, containing seven tiny jars for compost preparations; the other, a moon piece, like an amphora of wine, containing the many "documents" sent for the occasion. Musical scores, prayers, poems, and so forth, were sealed in the foundation under the altar.

Early in the 1970s, after I returned from a purgative year at the University of Lethbridge in Alberta, new elements came forward strongly in my work: a conscious modelling from the inside or from underneath—as in the Virgins of the Elk Dance—rather than building forms up by adding clay to the outer surface. This had obvious metaphysical overtones, i.e. "coming into form from the inside, from invisibility." Another was the appearance of the cluster, one piece made up of several separate pieces, such as Emerging Form (seven stages}, and the Six Grandfathers of the Flaming Rainbow Teepee, and the Program of Nine Dances, the triptych of three-piece drawings. I felt, and feel now, the correspondence of these inspirations to other forms: e.g. to poems made up of several words or lines; music of many notes, or few; and the new social art, a community which ripens out of developed individuals.

I've turned a lot to pinching pots also these past years. I like pinching because I touch every spot individually. There is nothing that is not intentional; the rim, every spot is pinched.

My work often comes out of the seasons, the cycle of festivals of the year. Here I have a thrown bowl with a wide flange, somewhat handled, with tenmoku glaze, then trailed with a white glaze. This Easter piece is Mary Magdalene wiping Christ's feet with her hair. The imagery of the hair, the feet, you wouldn't know what it was if I didn't tell you except that I've also written it on the back. It's a recent piece, done in that altered state of mind which I think of also as being characteristic of some of my work: the creative reach into a poetic imagery.

The seven "I Am's" came as a surprise, because they weren't at all planned ahead of time. They are inspired by the imagery of what is known as Christ's seven "I Am's": "I am the Light of the World," "I am the Door," "I am the Vine," "I am the Living Bread," "I am the Good Shepherd," "I am the Resurrection and the Life," "I am the Way, the Truth, and the Life." It's odd that these sayings should have been so alive in my unconscious that they came forth unbidden. I enjoy a religious temperament and the religious cultures of the planet, but I was never a diligent churchgoer. How did they come about? In 1964, the year *Centering* was published, I was very ill. I had to suffer major surgery both of my body and of my emotions. During my recovery, my convalescence, I was given a little booklet called *Meditation* by Friedrich Rittelmeyer. This little book was really about the Gospel of St. John and about the seven "I Am's." At that time, I received a great nurturing and healing. When I went to England and worked in the Curriculum Laboratory, I worked with teachers in clay and silkscreen and other arts. And I found the images of the vine and the door coming into my own work in silkscreen and poetry. Both of these seemed to capture an archetype in my unconscious, which was very nourishing to me. The idea of the vine had that sense of continuity, carrying life with continuity. And the image of the door and doorway evoked a kind of archway in which one stands, something open in front and behind, a kind of hinge that swings equally in both directions.

I remember distinctly that it was 1971, when I was at the farm. I was sitting at the desk by the window, looking out, pondering on "the door," thinking, "Guess I'll go into the studio and work with that image, the door." I did. Went over and made the door out of clay, which amused me because it was just a small door, with a doorknob I liked. Then I went on, made the vine, the good shepherd, which was quite a surprise because they were in low relief, and I had never worked with low relief. By the next day I had done them all: the bread; the Resurrection and the Life; the Light of the World; the Way, the Truth and the Life—which is the most difficult to read, I think. It's a heart-shaped head with just a faint physiognomy, faint eyes and mouth on a rough slab background. The face is marred by the accidents of the fire; it was too close to the shelf above. When I first saw it, I thought, "Oh, it won't do." But then I thought again, and it seemed appropriate that it should show signs of wear and tear. I think in a way that this piece is the most obscure because the image isn't all that clear. Also, the power of the image, heart-shaped head, and at the top of the head, the fontanelle, an opening... What is it that can stream in? It isn't like a block of wood or stone but something that is open to influences from the spiritual world. I learned later that that image, the heart-shaped head, is an ancient image on the planet. It has been used in petroglyphs across the Pacific, toward Asia 40,000 years ago.

So there they were, the seven "I Am's." I fired them and had no idea of their future or what would become of them. I took them around with me, showed them on any number of front lawns, on the running board of my car, whenever life offered some kind of place for them.

When I had my show in the fall of 1981 at Greenwich House, I took them there. The show closed on a Saturday, and on Monday I was to pack it up and take it home. That Sunday, I went to the Cathedral of St. John the Divine to attend a special celebration of the Earth community. All kinds of communities across the country were being represented there, the Findhorn people, and so on. After the service was over, I was introduced to the lady sitting next to me, who was Pamela Morton, wife of the Dean. I don't know how fate works, but when I said who I was, she recognized my name and said, "Oh, I've read your book *Centering*, and we carry it in our bookstore. Yes, we're great fans of pottery, you must meet my husband." Dean Morton came over and she said, "Look who we have here." Off we went to the deanery where he opened the dishwasher to show me all the mugs and things he had bought. He carried on about pottery, and I said, "Actually, I just had a show in New York." He was crushed. I said that the show was still up, but I had to pack it first thing in the morning. "Can you wait?" he asked me. "I'll come down first thing tomorrow to see it if that will be all right." I was dumbfounded. So Monday morning down he came to Greenwich House with a couple of young friends from the community get-together. When he saw the plaques, he said, "These belong in my cathedral. Could I hang them there?" Of course he could. I prevailed upon him to wait until the spring so I could do it with a lack of haste. "Yes," he said, "we'll have a party and you invite your friends." That's how the plaques came to live in the Cathedral of St. John the Divine for six months, beautifully placed, I thought, in the north transept. Projecting, even though they were low relief, across that space in a remarkable way. Now they're back at Rose Hall, hung differently as a cluster rather than in single file.[1]

In January of 1962, I received a phone call from Wesleyan University potters, asking me if I would give a talk at the regional meeting of the Connecticut Craftsmen to be held there in three weeks' time. I was utterly surprised to be called out of the blue like that. I learned that Francis Merritt (who had invited me to teach at Haystack) had recommended me as a possible speaker at this regional meeting. They didn't want a talk about markets or production problems, they wanted inspiration. I was asked to speak in a way that would be inspiring. How to do that? I decided I would share with them what had inspired me. In preparing the talk, I called it "Centering as Dialogue." Centering as dialogue comes from the relation between the clay and the hand, and the hand as a symbol for the whole person. It's not a symbol; it's attached to you, your hand, a part of wholeness, part of personal warmth, and other temperamental features expressed by one's hand, our uniqueness as well as our common characteristics. I prepared a talk about the relationship between the human being and the clay and the discovery that happens between them.

I delivered the talk on a snowy day in Middletown, Connecticut, and took a show of my work which I set up outside in the hall by the lecture room. After the talk, Will Lockwood, the editor of Wesleyan University Press, asked me if I could expand the theme of the talk into a book. I was astonished to be asked that since I had never written a book.

I had no status or reputation to be asked by a press if I could expand something into a book; it was really extraordinary. I thought I probably couldn't; I had said all I could say in that talk. Nonetheless, I returned to the press after six months of work with a manuscript two inches thick, over 300 pages long. Far from having no more to say, I found it was hard to shut me up. The editor

---

1. The "I Am's" have been returned to the cathedral.

and his staff were appalled at the length. They read through it quickly and asked me to cut it. There was too much personal material in it; for instance I had a long piece in it about John Cage and his importance historically. But I couldn't cut it down. It was like finding out a person was too big and he had to be cut down, like on the Procrustean bed (to make the person fit, he would cut off his legs); it was unthinkable to cut it. I had to wait many months before I could do it again within a smaller compass, to relive it, not by cutting, but by reducing. That's a photographic analogy, making the whole thing smaller but still whole.

One reviewer spoke of its sculptural quality. He said almost any sentence could be taken and, as it were, hung freely in the air, in space, for contemplation. The book has an aphoristic quality, a pithiness, a result perhaps of that reduction.

What happened in that first book was more of discovery, not just the initial talk that forms the basis for the first chapter. There were things I was asked for by former students, e.g., to talk about the way I taught, so there would have to be a chapter on pedagogy. Then I thought it would be interesting to have a chapter on poetry as a centering discipline and use my own poems. I found that these gave rise to not-so-obvious chapters like "Centering as Transformation," and the final chapter, "Ordeal by Fire." Ordeal by fire means evolution of person. It was in the Middle Ages when they would have the fire trial, to see how much heat a person could stand. That's how I think of life—how much heat can you stand? Particularly emotional experience, the astral experience being as intense as fire. Life has a way of preparing encounters for one with intense emotional experience which, if the fires are safely suffered through, has a purifying effect on one's organism. Our selfhood evolves in relation to the amount of reality we can bear. Not to resist but to receive it, to metabolize it so that the trials of life don't sit like a big wad in your stomach. It becomes part of your spiritual metabolism. When I say "spiritual" I don't mean it isn't physical. It has an additional effect on one's qualities of soul. At the end of that chapter of wrestling with the daimonic in *The Crossing Point*, I recount a dream in which there is a fire in the house in which I'm staying. I and a companion pack our bags and leave, but a friend, someone I know, stays there. Watching from outside. I see the fire approaching, going through the house, through the person, through the pots. And yet nothing is destroyed, I go back, and the friend who stayed through says, "Everything is still here, only the colors have deepened." And it was so. That's the ordeal by fire, if you're only able to go through it.

The last chapter of *Centering* is a long poem called "Recovery of the Child in Manhood."[1] This poem is a development from the process of doing the book. I let it happen, I let it be. The basic image of saving the inner child in manhood is the same image as that of the meristem that I mentioned in an earlier chapter of *Centering*. The meristem is that undifferentiated part of the plant which contains the possibility of growth, what you might call the growing tip. The meristem is in even the oldest oak, the growing tip, the possibility of creative development. By analogy, in the human being, we age toward childhood through the recovery of the child.

The next book, *The Crossing Point*, takes its title from a point in the geometric figure of the lemniscate. In doing the work with Olive Whicher, this figure became very important to me. I learned that there was a kind of geometric form which is expressed in the plant. It is the lemniscate, which is not a line but a plane, a ribbon. *Lemnis* means "ribbon." You have a figure eight made from a ribbon, with two surfaces. The genius of this form is that, if you put your finger on the outside of the top loop and come around through the crossing point, you find yourself on the inside of the bottom loop. What you have is a form with continuity between the

---

1. This poem has been reworked as "Recovery of the Child in Adulthood," and appeared in *Imagine Inventing Yellow* in 1991.

outside and inside, which we so often make a polarity instead of a continuum. The crossing point where the loops cross (and sometimes in a plant it's only one cell wide) is where the cells are undifferentiated. That's before they turn into, say, a root moving downward or a shoot moving up. By analogy, with a human being, there is a crossing point in the area of the heart. The bottom loop is where we're weighted, our gravity, and then we go up and out— into imagination, into intuition, and vision. We don't lose contact with the Earth. We don't have to decide between the practical and the visionary because we are both. We must always remember that and be faithful to it, not be talked out of it by ignorant teachers who would try to represent us as being less paradoxical than we are. Paradox is the heart of the matter, the heart's thinking.

The Crossing Point was a quite different kind of book than *Centering*. It was a collection of talks I'd given in a seven-year period between 1964 and 1971. It also has pictures of my pots, which is important to me because, since I'm asked to say things, I may be thought of more as a talker than a potter. I have to make it clear that that is not how I experience myself. That's why I bring my pots and set them around the hall when I'm asked to talk, so that my groundedness can be experienced at the same time my verbal imagination might be out front. Their function reinforces people in their awareness of how history is made, out of individual human beings doing things. It matters who and where we are. My little introduction is called "Who We Are." It's meant to be a statement of support for that feeling of how much we matter.

This is how *Toward Wholeness* came to be. I received a letter from Bert Lasky of Agathon Books, saying that Schocken Books was interested in the possibility of doing a book on Rudolf Steiner and education. Was I prepared to do it? I didn't know. I thought: "The only way to find out is by starting." My preparation for doing such a book was my years of hanging in with the Rudolf Steiner School in New York City and with Green Meadow School in Spring Valley, about a dozen miles from the

Stony Point community. I had done some reading of Steiner's lectures on education and had spent some time with the Camphill community and school for children. In a way I thought I wouldn't be the wrong person to write such a book because I had sympathy and I also had perspective. I was hopeful that it would receive attention, that it would stimulate an awareness of the values of that approach to education, which is that education is not just for schools, but for communities as well. It's a conception of the lifelong role of education.

For the next four years I wrote that book. I interviewed two big schools in California: Highland Hall in North Hollywood, and the Waldorf School in Sacramento. I sent chapters to the editor, and at the end I was really surprised when they said they couldn't use it. I had found their response quite encouraging but, when push came to shove, they found it "too philosophical." That was their charge. All right. But one of the features of the book is not just how they do it in a Waldorf school, but what ideas and assumptions underlie those techniques, what conception of the child underlies their approach to early childhood education. Those are the questions I wished to answer because those are the questions I asked. I sent the book to Wesleyan University Press, which had published my other books.

After *Toward Wholeness* had come out, I was driving home on the northwest extension of the Parkway on a beautiful afternoon. From off somewhere came a voice saying: "Now the next book to do would be a philosophy of adult education." I said, "Wait a minute ... wait a minute, I don't want anymore. I've had enough. Leave me be."

Like *Toward Wholeness, The Public School and the Education of the Whole Person* was published in 1980. I got a letter from Verlyn Barker, someone I didn't know, who was head of the United Church Board of Homeland Ministry in New York City. He said that this organization planned to do a series of booklets on the public schools, which would serve as discussion material for the congregations of the church. The feeling was that there was a deplorable apathy about public schools, and a way was needed to enliven interest in them. They got the idea of creating these booklets that would be circulated and used for discussion. They asked me to do the philosophical one, to be called *The Public School and the Education of the Whole Person*. That was the title they gave me. It was almost impossible to think how to go about doing this, beside the fact that I know little about public schools. But they said not to worry; I should do something that would be the underpinnings. So the day came when I just had to start doing it, sit down at the typewriter, put my fingers on the keys, and say "All right now." It started in the way I often seem to start, with the words themselves, the meaning of public school, of education, what means "the whole person." When we ask what we're talking about, we begin to unlock the experiences that are contained, packaged in these words. For words can be just like Hurrah words, just expressions of enthusiasm. If you want to know what something is, you can pause and meditate on the word, as I have done, on such words as *Art, Religion, Science, Person, Theory*. So I wrote this in a few weeks and enjoyed doing it because, in a way, I didn't have any idea of how to do it. So I just did it, let my fingers do the writing, trusting my process, trusting that meaning would flow through my fingers, a part of wholeness.

In the ordinary daily mind, to write on such a subject would take a lot of specific preparation: outlining, arranging, and so forth. I needed to use another part of the mind to approach such a subject—that's what I mean when I say I let my fingers do the writing. I permitted another part of myself to be the guide in that respect. I did very little filtering; I just wrote it down and left it in. There were religious passages. That's the way it is—you can't talk about education of the whole person without thinking about "the truth and the life." And that got me into a passage about the "I Am's." It's all very powerful, controversial material if you look at it soberly. And if you look at it ecstatically, it's just fine; it is the way I was looking at it. So I took it to Verlyn Barker and Douglas Sloan, from Columbia Teachers College, who were also on the committee, and they loved it! They said it was light years beyond what they'd hoped for. I asked, "What about this part here? What about that?" They said, "That will promote discussion." In every case the things I thought were problematical they assured me were just what they wanted. I allowed the overall religious light in which the whole thing is seen, to be changed somewhat for the comfort of readers who might not be able to imagine a cosmic Christ. In a way I think it's the best writing I've ever done. I didn't struggle with it; I just wrote it, and it fell into place. It drew me out in a way I just allowed, that's why I think it may be the best writing—it seemed to have an order and flavor in itself, a quality from within, a "Wholeness."

Part of the reason for the book *Toward Wholeness* was to provide something for the American friends interested in schooling for the child and adolescent. Waldorf education is an import, and many of its teachers and purveyors are European, German and Swiss, Dutch and English. They bring a style to it and an approach that is different from the American approach to things, which tends to be a bit more crude and open and open-hearted, you might say irreverent. Often people have trouble relating to Waldorf schools because they seem old-fashioned and odd. I wanted to write something that would indicate to people what this American felt. I even took teacher training at the New York school to get a better, more intimate understanding of the experience of the teacher, rather than just reading about it. That was one motivation, to tell my American friends who might be confused about their particular relationship to Steiner's work. The education which came to these shores brought us a great deal. But it not only brought something, it came to receive something too; we must look at this. We must not stand around quaking and tongue-tied but give it what we have and what it needs: a place in our culture.

> > > > >

I would like to tell you how the voice of Rudolf Steiner entered my life. I didn't go looking for it; it came to me and stayed there. Like a good friend, because of its vitality and the imaginative quality inherent in it.

When I went to Black Mountain College, I went with Bill Levi and his daughter, Estelle, who was then seven. In 1949, we took a leave from Black Mountain to go to Europe and, when we were in the south of France, we found a school for Estelle. We went to England for the spring months and were searching for a school where Estelle might be able to be with children her own age. This search took me to the Ministry of Education where I was given a number of brochures on childhood education. One, from Michael Hall, a Rudolf Steiner school, caught my attention because it was different from the others. It talked about childhood education, about the seven-year rhythms, the physical changes, and changes in the child's consciousness. It talked about creative and artistic learning, in addition to participating in the arts. It wasn't the right place for Estelle since she was only going to be there a few months, but I never forgot the description of that school in England. Years later, when I came upon Rudolf Steiner's work in America, it wasn't surprising to me. It was like picking up a dropped stitch, then knitting it into the fabric.

Two sources were feeding this material into my life. One was David Tudor, whom I have mentioned, a remarkable person and musician with whom I lived for more than a decade. He gave me a book of collected lectures of Steiner in translation. I found my own way into the substance of Steiner's philosophy of education, which then became an independent interest. In Stony Point we lived a dozen miles from Spring Valley, where there was an outstanding concentration of persons and work connected to the anthroposophy of Rudolf Steiner. That was the second source. It was at Spring Valley that I first learned of Camphill. During a

summer conference, Karl König, founder of the Camphill movement, came to give a lecture cycle on Sensology. Not of the five or
six or seven, but of the twelve senses. That caught my attention
more than just a little. The next year he returned to give a lecture
cycle on The Word, and again it was an extraordinary experience.
Koenig was a medical doctor and a musician. He introduced
Steiner's work in curative education, working with sick and
handicapped children. And then he turned to the gradual development of communities for adults, because when handicapped
children grow up and finish high school, then what? The concept
of the village as a working community with handicapped adults
was first described to me at those summer sessions. It contained
another feature, that of a new social impulse. The Camphill
movement was meant to represent another kind of social impetus,
a living and working together of human beings not only of different color, or race, or gender, but of different developmental
capacities, giving to each what was needed.

What was it about this new educational and social impulse
which attracted my attention? I had given up on conventional
education years before when I left the University of Chicago and
went to Black Mountain. Then, at Black Mountain, there was this
collapse of experimental education because of the instability of
community. What was it that so enlivened my interest again?
There was that approach all the way through to the wholeness of
the human being in Steiner's education, and the Camphill movement reconnected with that fundamental search in my life—the
hunch that there was still the possibility of connecting our learning and our living with more accuracy to the human being. And
to our mutual needs, not only community but also to the individual in relationship to the Earth, in relationship to the heavens.

What I wanted in my life was to live with others in an open-
ended way, not as a conclusion but as a beginning to consciousness. Rudolf Steiner's refrain: "O man, know thyself"—this was
the Sphinx's reply to Oedipus in some memorable encounter in

the desert of Egypt. In the classroom and in Camphill villages, the sense of community, the sense of *being* itself, is present. When you think of that as a voice of love and commitment to love, to brother-and-sisterhood, there is something added. And isn't that what they call synergy? When energies come together, there is an added quality, the whole being more than the sum of its parts. So it was and is with the Steiner schools and at Camphill. There is a sense of community being which supports and sustains our life and our work, even when our feelings as students or workers become unsure, uncertain, full of doubt, anguish, misery, or weakness of one kind or another. In earlier years, when this would happen, as at Black Mountain, people just left. Their questioning didn't let them stay and seek, but they left because the answer wasn't there. And likewise, at the Stony Point community in my own life.

In the Camphill communities one finds another kind of "glue" holding things together, so to speak. Like in a marriage, one looks for a kind of moral elasticity which allows for stress and change without rupturing the relationship. I have come to think of it as a kind of fine oil which allows the parts to move within a form, within a social form. A willingness to imagine and create new social forms is a social art.

One of the problems with being a Christian today is that some of the words seem dead. We don't know what anything means anymore. My way of finding out is to go through the words to an image which gives a clue to what the words mean. We learn that *Christos* means "The Anointed." What does that mean? There isn't anybody "anointed" in Idaho I've ever heard of. Anointed with what? Oil. Well, when you put oil on other things like paper or cloth, it makes them translucent so light can pass through. More than that, if it's the finest oil, it's used in the finest mechanisms. In watches, the finest oil is used to permit the smooth running of a complex entity, many little parts that move. It is the finest oil which permits all of us parts to move in relation to one another without abrasion. That's how I manage with language that has such tradition to it. You can't write off the tradition but you can find your own relation to it, which seems authentic and has a future in it.

In Camphill village where I live, I'm a household helper. I have created a pottery both for myself and for the villagers in the community. And I've started a little gallery where I exhibit creative activity from anyone in the community. I carefully avoided the word "art" because when you use it, the arguments begin: Is it or ain't it? If it isn't art, what is it doing here, et cetera. I call it creativity, and that covers it; it can go beyond good or bad. It enlarges the community's consciousness of itself. Right now I'm doing a poetry course with the farmers, the young women and young men who are in the biodynamic, agricultural training course or who are in charge of the sowing and reaping of the gardens and the fields. They asked me if I could meet with them once a week and open them up to poetry. We meet for half an hour every Friday morning. They're so busy that they have to get back to the milking machine or whatever, but they are starting to experience themselves as potential poets. They're beginning to have that experience. We did a sensory experiment last Friday on the room we were in. When they begin to write down their observations, the images begin to come. They're more open to spontaneous kinds of phrasing and the music, things which are in poetry. That's the way I try to do it, not to tell them what poetry is and have them remember what I said, but to get them into the process of perceiving. It could be the simplest thing. William Carlos Williams' poem about the red wheelbarrow: "So much depends / upon / a red wheel / barrow / glazed with rain / water / beside the white / chickens." He lifts that image into the imagination where it lives on another level as well as: "Just look at that old wheelbarrow. It's all wet and there are chickens nearby...." Something else happens, and that's why Steiner says that perhaps art, and poetry as an art, are ways to initiation.

There are many ways, but art as one way brings you to supersensible experience as the senses are lifted into the imagination. There are special kinds of cognition available to us through color. I am just beginning to have in my own life real experiences where color is itself a path of cognition. It's not just talk, like, oh, I love color. One can feel oneself changed in one's consciousness. I have had a showing of my dry pastels and will this winter share my paintings with watercolor. Today I wrote up material from a morning session with the farmers on poetry. I couldn't bear the black and white of the pen and paper. I was so hungry for color I had to get my paints out. (I carry a small traveling watercolor set in my purse.) I could tell something was changed by giving myself permission to do that, that something was relaxing, completed, realized, stepped further, or true. A page without color is not true because life without color doesn't exist. Color has a being, an energy, a presence, a spiritual nature. By spiritual I mean that it's more than the chemical components of color; it affects the experience at the core. There are exercises developed under the influence of Rudolf Steiner where one works with a single color.

The farmer men and women wanted to do something for a couple of their members who just got married. They wanted to make a poem but were naturally fearful because they had never done such a thing before. I suggested they make some thing like a photo album where memories would be shared: the way things looked, things that had happened. Only, in words. I suggested we do it right then in class to see if it was a good idea, if there was anything in it. I did it too as I always share in class assignments. Well, they were surprised at what they did, by the flow of feeling and imagery. I wrote their (our) poems on a big roll of paper like a scroll. At the wedding party, the horizontal scroll was unrolled. As each poem came into view, the "poet" read it out to the audience who were sitting on hay bales in the big yard. Something had really happened, and everyone could feel it. A change in consciousness. That's what it's about, isn't it? To open up to the fact that we live in poetry. That's the crossing point, we live right in it. Carried across the threshold, as it were, by imagination; carried like a bride, by our radiant lover, into the new home. Outwardly the same old home but inwardly differently lit, differently experienced.

> > > > >

I remember the day, probably more than twenty years ago, when I went to my studio to work and stood momentarily gripped by a deep longing I didn't understand. I want to live the religious life, I was saying. What could I mean? Did I want to become a nun? What was that inner question all about? The angel on the compost pile said not to worry about it.

Two things I want to tell you: to begin with the word *religious*. It comes from the Latin, *re* and *ligio*, "again" and "to connect." To reconnect: the human spirit with spirit in the universe. To come into life from the inside. To be fed by the clay as by a divine soup! The full dish of animate clay, as I wrote somewhere.

Then: I had a big dream about language and its importance. I was talking with John Cage, the composer-philosopher-friend. He was drinking a glass of water and asking about the subject of my book. I don't remember now what angered me but I struck the glass from his hand, only to see it reappear filled with water in his fingers. I walked away. David Tudor followed me, saying he could help me with my book, that he was "clairvoyant about the future of society." "Yes," he said, "it hangs upon linguistics." Charles Olson said I should take this as a "directive." Apparently my unconscious has done so. The dream knew it long ago.

Now I can live the religious life wherever I am. A religious community feels the presence in its daily life of something more than the peeling of potatoes or the hoeing of corn. These are actually implicit acts of praise. It's as if our raking were scratching the backs of the gods. We can live inwardly and outwardly, like a clay vessel. In small specific ways to live the spirit of wholeness, as well as in the grandeur of visions.

The future? "I wouldn't worry about that if I were you."

Black Mountain College
A Personal View of Creativity

Black Mountain College,
a radical vision and
venture

on this occasion
we honor it
remember it
celebrate its continuing
relevance to the human spirit
in its quest for creative freedom
and depth in learning.

I will talk about the impact of Black Mountain on my life, in order to witness the formative power of an educational impulse, to suggest values and their consequences. My purpose is to invoke a certain spirit, to create an atmosphere, which feels like the Being we know as Black Mountain College. She was born in controversy and died in controversy, splendid in the between, as she inspired and shattered dreams of liberation and fulfillment. She lay on her side as the hills did across from Lake Eden, female in form. She hooted with the owls, and sat at peace with whatever her fate was to be.

I'll start with a short poem written at Black Mountain College in 1952, the year I started working with clay as well as words, celebrating a basic transformation in my life—integrating the nonverbal experience of pottery into my life of language.

Sun-up /
over the valley's lip a running glaze.
Lake, crazed and curdled.

Sun-down / and
the dense rim fires
nut-black bone-brown.

Stoneware is the night,
its granite foot, aside, the hills,
trimmed sills and shallows, O bene,
bene,
blessed be the jars that
burn with day, turn smack
center on the whirring dark.

It's a love poem, isn't it—the face of the beloved seen every-where one looks in nature: "over the valley's lip," "stoneware is the night,"—homage to the potters who taught me: Robert Turner, Karen and David Weinrib, Warren McKenzie, Dan Rhodes, Peter Voulkos. Homage to the landscape, to the cosmos beyond landscape, the "whirring dark." A sense of union, of connection. The nonverbal ecstasy put into words.

I arrived from the University of Chicago for my first visit and interview for a place on the faculty in July, 1945. About 50 students, 15 faculty. "Which is the Black Mountain?" I asked at mealtime on the dining-hall porch, looking out and up at the Smokies. The students interviewed me sitting on the floor in their studies. Max Dehn, the math prof, took me on a walk to the pasture high up and got me back late for my lecture, "Irony in Joseph Conrad and Thomas Hardy," as I recall. I ran through the gathering audience on the way to one of the lodges, where the talk was to take place, to change my clothes and get my notes. I was attracted by the rustic vitality of the environment and the intense faces.

I was offered a job to teach English (I called it Reading and Writing) and came to work in September, with Bill Levi and his seven-year-old daughter Estelle and cocker spaniel Blackie. Bill would teach philosophy and social science. His lecture to the community was on Whitehead and the philosophy of organism. The college was in a fragile emotional state, having just lost one of its central figures, Robert Wunsch, in a particularly painful way.

In 1950 Bill and Estelle left. In 1951 I left, both of us deeply shaken by our inability to keep our marriage together and by our inability to stay faithful to the college that had inspired our best efforts, the Black Mountain we are celebrating here this weekend.

Was it the Demon Lover, who teased us from our conventional middle-class commitments, our spouses and children so to speak, parents and colleagues at conventional institutions, and took us into a radiant sailing on the onyx blue sea, and in due course "brake that gallant ship in twain, and sank her in the sea," as the old ballad tells?

What did the college call for? AN ALTERED STATE OF CONSCIOUSNESS! Not the same old competitive combative ambitious materialistic stench. It smelled good, fresh and inviting. The problem was that though it struck fire with the secret vision of possibilities for education and community and artistic development and human creativity we carried deep within us, we hadn't developed many habits that made possible a steadfast commitment to process; through thick and thin, sickness and health, better and worse. Many of the old habits we who came to Black Mountain brought with us carried within them the shadows of adversarial relationships: "objecting to," "resisting," "fighting against." All in the name of idealisms that had been armored in those days. That's why the battles were holy wars, giving no quarter. Some of the old-timers, when I got there in 1945, Anni Albers and Molly Gregory, knew about "staying power," and "containment," and finding the "third way" out of conflict between two points of view or two policies. We were called to a new consciousness, and we felt the thrill of a new vision—something generous, resourceful, contemporary, witty, informed, visionary, and grounded in the daily work we chose to share: doing the dishes, cleaning the bathrooms and toilets, mowing the grass, getting in the hay, getting in the coal, building the studies building, minimum house, the science building, the pottery studio, the music practice room.

It was this new consciousness that changed my life, taking me free of the pattern of divided loyalties that most schools foster: either intellectual or artistic, either visionary or practical, either private or social, either this subject or that—anthropology or creative writing, poetry or politics, painting or farming, history or philosophy, theater or government. The threefoldness of the Black Mountain educational thrust brought me into a current of living and learning that was new: community building, artistic participation in studio experience, intellectual study. It was a new strain of seeding: it grew into twenty-five years of inquiry into themes of WHOLENESS, in four books: beginning with *Centering: In Pottery, Poetry and the Person*, 1964, and moving on through *The Crossing Point*, 1973, and *Toward Wholeness: Rudolf Steiner Education in America* and *The Public School and the Education of the Whole Person*, 1980. It was this new consciousness of bearing within ourselves the pattern that connects, to use Gregory Bateson's phrase. A participatory consciousness, to use Owen Barfield's phrase. It is actually a kind of religious consciousness in that it inspires awe before the connections we feel between persons, between persons and nature, and between our speaking mouths and the silence at the back of our throats—the big silence out of which everything comes. I often these days ask my classes to ponder on the question of where our words are before we speak them. We do not rehearse what we will say to one another as we meet here. We open our mouths and the speech comes. The so-called speech organ trips the silence into syllables, out of an unconscious nonverbal creative source. It's enough to make mystics of us all.

So what did I learn there, in what I call my post-university education? I have mentioned the three elements of community, study, and artistic studio experience. Community as process: the need for goodwill and patience as well as passion—risking one's creativity, seeing one's original face for the first time, not Helen Frankenthaler, not Georgia O'Keeffe, not Lucy Rie nor Mary Frank, nor Denise Levertov or Adrienne Rich. Can I bear to be called by my name and to stand in the shine? Can I bear to take on my identity— wherever it leads, shedding fantasy like an old coat, taking on the NOW, just now: I AM HOLDING THIS BRUSH AND PAINTING THIS COLOR—NO WHY, JUST IN PRAISE OF ISNESS. To learn to take my losses without being permanently disabled. To let the new life, new growth, quicken in time and show its original face! It takes time. It has taken time. TO PRAISE IS THE WHOLE THING.

There is a Rilke poem, one of the sonnets to Orpheus, which has helped me a lot to transform an unbearable sense of loss into something like gratitude. "To praise is the whole thing" is its first line, in the Robert Bly translation.

> To praise is the whole thing. A person who can praise
> comes toward us like ore out of the silence
> of rock. The heart, that dies, presses out
> for others a wine that is fresh forever.
>
> When the god's image takes hold of us,
> our voices never collapse in the dust.
> Everything turns to vineyards, everything turns to grapes,
> made ready for harvest by our powerful south.
>
> The mold in the catacomb of our memory
> does not suggest that our praising is less,
> nor deny that the gods cast shadows.

> We are friends who do not go away,
> who still hold through the doors
> of the tomb trays of shining fruit.

The way I would put it is that we are not in a game called nostalgia—but look through a transparency of the heart to archetypal images of a true story. We have done our share of grousing, of grieving, of despairing over the mortality of the living form—but at the same time we serve an ongoing liveliness of imagination, an ongoing vision of sweetness and mirth and heartburn—we stand in the door between the present and the past, holding in our arms trays of shining fruit in a new weather of perceived continuity, of commitment, of secret love. "We are friends who do not go away / but who still hold through the doors / of the tomb trays of shining fruit."

Another Rilke poem rounds us off:

> I live my life in growing orbits
> which move out over the things of the world.
> Perhaps I can never achieve the last,
> but that will be my attempt.
> I am circling around God, around the ancient tower,
> and I have been circling for a thousand years.
> And I still don't know if I am a falcon,
> Or a storm, or a great song.

When Black Mountain adjourned, in 1956, I didn't think I could bear it. Why? I can still hear myself saying, as I strode up the hill past the studies building toward the wood shop and print shop, talking on the way earnestly with student friends: in the midst of a troubled time, difficult faculty and community meetings—struggling to understand, to persevere, to survive, to flourish and blossom and bloom—I can hear myself saying, "If we can't do it here, where can we do it? There is nothing in the way.

No administration, no bureaucracy, no deans, no department politics. If we can't do it here...." And my assumption was implicit: namely, that with the old obstacles out of the way, there was nothing to keep us from success in our endeavors to create an original and fruitful human educational community.

Ah, yes, we did the best we could. I see it now. We lit our little light on the darkling plain of higher education and human values and it has not gone out. Look at us here. And listen to the Black Mountain legend as it grows like the kudzu vine. There was a truth that brought us there and sustained us through heartbreak and collapse and poverty. It shines through the archetypal golden seed and in all its scattered progeny.

You can see the final adjournment of Black Mountain College also in a creative image. It is one I met recently in a show of work by Ariel, paintings and drawings and sculptures. She called her show EXPLOSIONS. And she wrote

> THESE ARE EXPLOSIONS, IN THE SENSE THAT
> A BUCKEYE TREE OR A WORK OF ART IS A LONG
> SLOW EXPLOSION THAT BEARS IN ITS
> FINAL FORM
> THE CHARACTER OF TENSION AND RELEASE
> OF ITS ENGENDERING.

Black Mountain College had its engendering in the imaginative intelligence of John Andrew Rice. It bore within it the intention to avoid becoming an "institution." At one time Rice said he thought the college should disperse every ten years into smaller units, each of which could develop its own educational identity. This was to avoid too much stability. It was to be faithful to the chaos out of which creativity constellates. There is a view of creativity shining through the fabric of Black Mountain which to me has the wisdom of the Fool—the wisdom of the Saint. It has affected deeply my own lifelong engagement with creativity as a Life Path.

Before I was really thinking consciously about this talk, someone asked me what I was going to talk about in San Francisco. "Grief and destruction," I responded, with a flavor of energy that took me aback and also my listener.Grief and destruction. The shadow of Black Mountain's light. A darkness that is actually part of a living light, in some mysterious way empowering it.

So much suffering, so many disasters, schisms, expulsions—the founder himself booted out, marriages down the drain. What sense did it make? So many pretensions: how could it be if we were all so talented and creative and informed and superior to other educational efforts, how come we couldn't keep our college together or our marriages?

Ahhhh, is that what you want to learn? How to keep things together? Is that the essence of creativity, of insight, of sensitivity, of wisdom? Surely the paraphernalia of conventional institutions exists precisely to keep them together, to provide stability and security against the weather of natural process. This stability and security can be the death forces that inhibit creative development. Most people want it that way, happy to settle for security at the cost of basic life energy. But the life story of Black Mountain contains elements not only of the Fool: innocent, inspired, maladapted, touching us with its foolish intimacy and personal aliveness, heedless of consequences, of rewards: no grades, no accreditation, no tenure, no real salary. Elements not only of the Fool, but of the Saint: living in poverty, in purity of purpose, and in a willingness to sacrifice. There wasn't enough income from student fees to continue, and Steve Forbes foreclosed. People stayed with the college when there was no reason to, except fidelity to their truest intentions. And a willingness not to be saved by recanting. The college in a way was sacrificed to the values of the culture: defeated, as it were, by money. The foundations that now give funds for research on Black Mountain would give us none when we needed it to survive. They like us dead better than they liked us alive.

.... a poem by Juan Ramon Jimenez

> I have a feeling that my boat
> has struck, down there in the depths,
> against a great thing.
>   And nothing
> happens!   Nothing … Silence … Waves
> —Nothing happens? Or has everything happened,
> and we are standing now, quietly, in the new life?

Let me describe briefly the new life that happened for me out of Black Mountain. I had come to Black Mountain out of reaction against conventional higher education, at the University of Chicago, where I was teaching English in the four-year college, one of Robert Hutchins' pioneering efforts. I had taken my Ph.D. in English at the University of California in Berkeley, and there had been stimulated by Hutchins' vision of the Intellectual Virtues. Teaching at Chicago, and meeting the students' obsession with passing exams and achieving professional status, I thought, "If these are the virtues, I would be better off damned." I had heard of Black Mountain in my undergraduate days at Reed College in Portland, Oregon. John Kelley, who had studied music at Black Mountain, transferred to Reed. He told me all about it and gave me a brochure with photos of students and teachers talking together on a building site—the studies building. I was deeply struck. The vision stayed with me. So, when the crisis occurred ten years later, I wrote to Black Mountain. Before I gave up higher education entirely, I thought I would try the other end of the stick.

I had been educated, as most of us have, to be an intellectual of the verbal type. I thought there were two kinds of people in the world: intellectuals and artists. No, three! Intellectuals, artists, and women. How to find my way? That and other hogwash got purged at Black Mountain. An imagery of wholeness began to develop. It found its shape in the experience of centering clay on the potter's wheel. Before we built the pot shop at Black Mountain (after Albers left), I had been opened to studio work in the wood shop, the printing shop, the dance studio, and in sharing work with my creative writing class. Theater also, as I translated a Satie play for a summer music festival, and translated and produced Cocteau's *Marriage on the Eiffel Tower*. And more.

CENTERING IS THE DISCIPLINE OF BRINGING IN RATHER THAN LEAVING OUT.

Work in the nonverbal arts healed that division so widespread in education between verbal and nonverbal experience. I have come to the view that all experience, all language, is nonverbal. Or, WHERE ARE THE WORDS BEFORE WE SPEAK THEM? And I developed a pilot program at Penland School of Crafts in 1966 called "Cross Over to a New View of Language, Verbal and Non-Verbal." The workshops I now give come under the umbrella of "Creativity in Clay and Word." Actually I have now added color to the mix. Departments of Interdisciplinary Studies are beginning to develop in some colleges. My work is beginning to find its new community. At the present moment I am teaching the winter term at the Institute for Culture and Creation Spirituality, under the direction of Matthew Fox, at Holy Names College in Oakland. "Clay, Color, and Words."

It may seem strange to put clay and words together, but my interest is not simply an accident of my own biography. There is an archetypal link between the two, which I will just hint at here. If you look at the accounts of creation in our Judeo-Christian scriptures, you will find in Genesis that we were made originally of clay, into which divinity breathed spirit. *SPIRITUS* is the Latin word for BREATH. Breath makes our bodyclay sacred. If you look at St. John's gospel in the New Testament, you will see "In the beginning was the Word." So now, which paper do you read? Are we clay or are we word? Ah, we are both: gravity bound, standing on the Earth, having the weight of clay, and at the same time weightless! Weightless in our thinking, our imagination, our dreaming. The clay gives us our physical shape, the word gives our interiority, our inner forming. Like germinating seeds, we grow in opposite directions simultaneously: rooted in the dark Earth, opening to the Sun's light. This polarity gives us our genius as human beings: to be both practical and visionary!

I left Black Mountain in 1951 and went to New York with David Tudor, the pianist who had come to Black Mountain to accompany the dancer Katherine Litz and to play the music of John Cage, Henry Cowell, Schoenberg, Webern, Boulez. It was through David that I came to translate Antonin Artaud's *The Theater And Its Double*, published by Grove Press in 1958. In New York were a band of sisters and brothers in the arts, and in 1954 some of us made a new community in Stony Point, 35 miles north of the George Washington Bridge, with the help of Paul Williams' support, enthusiasm, and abilities as an architect. When a student at Black Mountain, he had been the creative agent of Minimum House and the Science Building; he was also the student representative in all faculty meetings. The Gate Hill Community began with eight Black Mountaineers (Paul and Vera Williams, David and Karen Weinrib, John Cage, David Tudor, myself, and Patsy Lynch Davenport & family.) Soon other families joined, including Stan Vanderbeek, Black Mountain artist and farmer.

I made pots and taught evening session English courses at City College of New York, and made a garden, learning about compost and organic gardening, and herbs. My teaching at City College was strongly influenced by my Black Mountain experience. It was, first of all, personal. I made clay cups for my classes, and took them home-baked bread. It was independent of catalogue prescriptions. For example, I gave a course in the poetry of Gerard Manley Hopkins, certainly not listed. There's a lot you can do in the world once your field of vision opens up and your creativity is lit.

One of the things I enjoyed particularly at Black Mountain was the way we developed curriculum. At the opening of the term, we would all gather to hear what teachers were proposing to teach and what students wanted. This dialogue produced creative results. I remember the years I wanted to teach the works of Thomas Mann, of James Joyce, Shakespeare, or Greek Drama. Would there be any takers? What would the students ask for? Ah, writing, yes—and poetry. Then, working together through the year, we could discuss what we would like to do next.

Black Mountain was a liberal arts college, not an art school, though the studio arts gave it its particular buoyancy, I believe. There was no pressure on anyone to graduate, but if you wanted to go on to graduate school, we had a stiff preparatory program, which culminated in an oral exam by a specialist invited from the school of your choice. The students who graduated even without accreditation had no difficulty in continuing their academic work.

My own studies continued after Black Mountain, in dialogue with the potter's wheel, so to speak: Suzuki and Zen Buddhism, Jung and archetypal psychology, Martin Buber and Hasidic lore, Owen Barfield in the evolution of consciousness and the history of language, and Rudolf Steiner in education, biodynamic agriculture, sensory development, mental handicap, and the transformation of thinking into imagination, inspiration, intuition. I listened to a lot of music and pulled curtains on Merce Cunningham's dance tours! After the publication of *Centering*, I never returned to conventional academic employment, but made my living with free-lance workshops. The interdisciplinary flavor discovered at Black Mountain took stronger and stronger hold. It turned out to be prophetic.

I live now (for the past seven and one-half years) once again in community. It is called Camphill Village, in Kimberton, Pennsylvania, part of a worldwide movement of working communities with the mentally handicapped. We are about 120 souls, 40 of them disabled. Our work is biodynamic agriculture and gardening, and social therapy. The economics is a "needs" policy, very like Black Mountain. I have a pottery studio where I work and have open sessions with the community. I teach in our agricultural training program a course called "The Renewal of Art Through Agriculture," as a way of getting to living sources. I live in a group home with seven or eight others, and share in the cooking and family life. The personal creative work which is absorbing me most is painting. Acrylic on big pieces of paper or canvas. I will have a show in New York City in May at the Cathedral of Saint John the Divine. A set of seven ceramic plaques also hang in the Cathedral. In September at the Tampa Museum of Art in Florida there will be a show called "The Black Mountain Connection: Four Artists: Cage, Cunningham, Kremen, Richards." John Cage's drawings and watercolors, Merce Cunningham's drawings of insects, Irwin Kremen's collages, and my pots and paintings. Four of us, friends since Black Mountain. If an art museum in 1992 can draw an audience by billing an exhibit "The Black Mountain Connection: Four Artists," we must have done something right!

Can you see how the threads of life have spun out of the belly of Black Mountain these past thirty-five years since its adjournment? Community, art, study ... trying to work toward the sources of our freedom....

I thought I might end by saying something briefly about my current posture (to use Charles Olson's favorite image) in relation to education. I like the *Menschenschule*, the School of Life attempted in our rural Camphill communities. I am drawn to the vision and practice of Matthew Fox in his Institute for Culture and Creation Spirituality: working always toward Community, Deep Ecology, Deep Ecumenism, the Arts as Meditation (as Centering), New Forms of Worship, GeoJustice, Compassion Practicum, Dances of Universal Peace, Cosmology—inspired by the quizzical wisdom of Meister Eckhart and the mystical practice of Hildegard of Bingen; finding our way through the Praise, the

Grief and Destruction, the Creativity, to the Transformative: to Social Justice and Compassion.[1]

Our country is reasonably literate in a conventional sense. And yet it reeks of injustice, social suffering, poverty. Why? What are we not learning in school? We seem to have so much trouble relating openly to one another, really receiving one another, or a new idea. And so much trouble building a social organism that is both reasonably firm and inspiringly flexible. I have a couple of recent intuitions I will share with you: one has to do with handicap, one with painting.

What are the handicaps of the normal human being as we know ourselves in the community process? This is a question that has been with me since Black Mountain: what are the handicaps of the liberal intellectual? From what I know now, I would say that autism and hysteria are the illnesses that education could address. We could begin to think of the purpose of education as curative, or healing. We would think of our self-enclosure, our inability to respond, to connect, to experience the world of all beings as our autism, an illness inherent in our nature, and only aggravated by left-brain intellectual work. A spiritual awakening to the life in all things could be undertaken. For spirit is a capacity to relate to all things and all beings, not just the vested interests of humans.

And if we could see our inability to take form, our tendency to disperse, to thin out at the edges, to dissolve, as symptoms of hysteria, to be understood and worked with and overcome. To know ourselves and our handicaps could help us to be more realistic in our expectations, what we can hope for ourselves in this period of evolution—and what we need to learn, what we need to develop. A new and more imaginative picture of the cosmos will be the ground of our ecology.

---

1. Matthew Fox has now founded the University of Creation Spirituality, opening in Oakland, California, September 1996.

When I paint, I push the color around on the paper or canvas. The experience is of color and the energy of the brush. It is not drawing, it is painting. The color and the movement bring me close to the edge, where consciousness changes, and what lives on the other side of the senses comes through. Black Mountain shoved me up to the gate—like those Olympic downhill skiers crouched and trembling at the threshold—and forty years later I'm in the middle of a jump, learning what art is about.

"Why did Black Mountain fail?" I am asked. It didn't fail! It lived its life passionately and earnestly and because it was alive and not artificially preserved, then it ceased to exist as a body. How vividly it is living now in the imagination of persons!

"Apparently it is refreshing to hear that we don't have to be large, rich, funded, well known, successful in order to inspire and endure. In a society that promotes values of status, money, production, fame, we like to be told the legend of a college where the arts were central to its life, a college that was poor, confused, small, offbeat, and a college that drew creative people to it for no other reason than that they wanted to be there. A spirit drew them."[2]

Can there be another Black Mountain? Of course not. Black Mountain was specific, cultural, personal, and historical—once in an evolutionary history of 18 billion years, as Matthew Fox said. But there can be other experiences undertaken together by persons who want to create. Want to do physical work as well as administrative work as well as teach, want to live thriftily and imaginatively, want to make something NEW. Want to farm, want to work the land, want to attract artists (keepers of the soul) more than security forces (keepers of the body). Are willing to do without endowment, tenure, departments, accreditation, degrees. The body comes and goes, the spirit flies. Look at the SCATTERED

---

2. Quoted from "Black Mountain College: A Golden Seed," in *Black Mountain College Sprouted Seeds*, ed., Mervin Lane (Knoxville: University of Tennessee Press, 1990).

SEEDS. Black Mountain is infiltrating the cosmos, sending up its shoots of humor and seriousness and originality and affectionate disrespect.

Our closing focus can be again on the love poem with which we began:

HOMAGE

Sun-up /
over the valley's lip a running glaze,
lake, crazed and curdled.

Sun-down / and
the dense rim fires
nut-black, bone-brown.

Stoneware is the night,
its granite foot, aside, the hills,
trimmed sills and shallows. O bene,
bene,
blessed be the jars that
burn with day, turn smack
center on the whirring dark.

The Public School and the Education of the Whole Person

We do not scold the cock for calling dawn,
the cow for lowing when her day is done:
a time for rising, a time for bedding down,
a time for travelling to the town and home again.

Life has her seasons, teaches us her tides.
Says, "Wait! Reflect!" Says "Leap! Give all!"
We follow in her wake in little boats
getting the feel of currents as we ride.
We put to sea or seek the shore with equal joy.
We climb the mast or set the grate below.

Our song is deep within us for the work:
to keep the faith, to worship and to grow.
The Vine winds through us, spring and fall:
now lush in fruit, now wizened bough.

Wholeness we bear within us like a seed:
to die, to grow, to sleep and grow again.
It is the mystery of person and of world,
of inner fire and flavor and respect.
It is our name, our home, our neighborhood.
We are its art. Its forming makes us good.

The schooling that we seek is full within.
It rises to the surface as we move.
It has the face of angels, human speech.
All present borderlines are lit with warmth
like autumn maples tilting in the sun.

Our planet is our school, and far beyond:
our church, our shop and study, and our fields.
We are all learning to awake:
awake in dream, in meditation and in prayer.
Inspired awake! Inspirited awake!
We feel it thus: one mighty school, the teaching everywhere.

M.C.R.
October 24, 1979

What is Our Concern?

Education is in crisis. Public schools are losing public confidence and its support. Public schools are losing students. What is wrong? Or perhaps nothing is wrong! Perhaps these are symptoms of growth, of needed change. Old forms die when life goes out of them. The message may be that new growth is on the way. Perhaps the human spirit is ready to take a new step into selfhood, and is outgrowing institutions which cannot help it on its way.

One can get the impression when one goes to school that there is some kind of social organization one is supposed to fit into. Pressures and controls and penalties and rewards are steadily applied. The mood is stifling. Is this what going to school is about? Is this what it is to become a human being and make one's offering? One gets the impression that there are certain kinds of people in the world, certain roles available to one: thinkers, artists, do-ers. Athletes, priests, women. So we have a verbal curriculum

78

for "intellectuals," art classes for "the gifted," vocational schools for "workers." Women stay fairly confused. Athletes make their millions and retire to do TV commercials. Priests receive special benefits. The person is treated like a sack of aptitudes that are to be sorted out, "modified," and put to work. This materialistic mood is intolerable to the human soul, and it withdraws its support.

Teachers become discouraged, students lose energy and often drop out for their own souls' sake, parents don't vote public funds because the system isn't working. And the society of educated adults proceeds in its own way toward self-destruction, which it calls security. Outmoded science prepares us for annihilation. Outmoded pragmatism prepares us for despair. The new science finds consciousness permeating matter. The new empiricism finds that experience drinks from deep inner springs. "Whole," "holy," "heal" all come from the same root. It may be the root from which new educational forms may grow.

What are schools supposed to do? Teach reading, writing, arithmetic? Farming, mechanics, carpentry? Joy, compassion, imagination, diligence, goodwill? Social conformity? Social originality? Independence? Balance? Personal authenticity? A sense of connection? A sense of meanings? Can home, church, and school cooperate in a review of essential values?

What answers are ripening in the creative spirit of the human person? What questions rise like flowering stems, casting their seed for the next season of our growth?

Entering the Temple of the Question

What is a Person?
What is Wholeness?
What is Education?
What is a School for Persons Who Wish to Live and Grow toward Wholeness?

Perhaps we do not know the answers to these questions. And perhaps it is good we do not know. Perhaps it is desirable to learn to live in the question, in an ongoing inquiry, and relationship, and journey. Perhaps a question is a good kind of activity to be able to live in, rather than to be uneasy and perhaps feel that answers are better than questions. Questioning and answering can be pictured as a kind of breathing in and out, a total process which sustains; or like the two chambers of the heart, pulsing rhythmically in a continuous single circulation. Each is, in this light, an aspect of the other, of the whole. So when we take on a question, let us feel the steady beat of an answering response implicit within it, and be unafraid. At the same time that we ask what to do, we are doing something. So we will begin by feeling how the answering too is a continuous relationship, growing and changing, as the question continues to open up in new ways as situations change and history continues to unfold. Some wise wit once said, "It isn't the problems we should worry about, it's the solutions!" Another kind of wisdom comes from the antiphonal form of the Psalms, as if this dialogue between questioning and responding is like a flow of sap, an archetypal resource in our being. So perhaps our first meditation should be to enter into the temple—a sacred space—with awe and reverence and attentive listening—and with our bodies open to respond from their midmost point.

We begin our inquiry with a candid commitment to a certain way of asking. It is the Way of Truth and of Life. This is the Door through which we enter the temple of our inquiry.

Let us keep our ear and our listening open to the full image of a schooling for all persons in their wholeness, and not be tempted to leave out or to compromise any part of that full image. So let us then dream together a bit: the spirit will speak to us of its hopes and idealism and longing, of its terrors. What does our human soul dream of for itself, and what does our body need for its health and wholeness?

Dreams as Guides to New Ideas

Dreams may be the doorway through which spirit reaches and enters in the familiar dress of ordinary life. We long for living truth and justice and peace, for living words between people, for loving generosity and patience and steadfastness, for meaningful work, and for warm humor, and we dream of a Sky turned to Ocean and a Heavenly Fish leaping through its Waves! We long to be of service, and we dream of an oak whose heart is open like petals. We long for practical knowledge, and we dream of a hand-made bowl overflowing with milk and the milk is running into the field where it is being lapped up by deer and the antlers of the deer are harps vibrating with song and along the singing antlers elemental beings are dancing with diamonds between their funny teeth and the foundation of a building is sinking into the field where the deer are lapping and the devas are dancing, and walls are rising and particular practical arts of civilization have begun: Here is the miller, here the smith, here the mason, here the gardener and here the child and here the priestess and here the donkey. The dream wakes into consciousness. Where do we want to begin? The milk is running over, the Earth is making new foundations for us, the people are walking in.

What do we wait for? We wait for imagination to take us free of our habits. We wait to imagine that we might actually make something we like, make something new and good and decent, make a difference, do something, feel good about the world, feel in harmony with ourselves, be co-creators in a courageous and forward-looking community—keeping the faith in all kinds of weather. We wait to feel supported by others.

Our second meditation then might be an exercise in imagination. Suppose a creature from another planet were to knock at your door, and you answer the knock, and the creature asks who you are. In the course of identifying yourself, you say not only that you are Deborah Anderson or Jack Stewart, but also that you are a human being, a person, with this name. And suppose your visitor asks you what that means? What is a human being, who is a person with a name? Here is, probably, the heart of our inquiry, and, therefore, where it ought to start. I say "start" in the way a sun might be said "to start." That is, it "starts" by shining out in all directions. It will touch all the rest of what we say, just as the Sun touches the Earth everywhere. The way we feel about who a Person is, really, is the cornerstone of our schooling. The way we answer what a Human Being is predicts the education we are likely to permit. Maybe we have not thought about these questions very consciously. Maybe we don't really know what we think.

Perhaps the next meditation might be to gather into consciousness, as best we can, the assumptions and values we have. The place where consciousness and unconsciousness meet is another kind of Doorway. It is a fertile ground for self-knowledge. When we get closer to the ideas we have that we may not know we have, then we can begin to be more awake to ourselves. Choices can then begin to occur. Self-knowledge is where charity begins: at home. It is the threshold of love. Until we cross this threshold, of loving self-knowledge, we cannot go through The Door.

Threefold Person and Continuity Through Change

In the archway of that Door, we stand as Human Persons: Spirit, Soul, and Body. This threefoldness creates our wholistic approach to education. We want to be sure that the human being is spoken to in all three realms. Our Spirit is manifest in our individuality. Our Soul is manifest in our thinking and our feeling and our willing to do and to make and to ask and to express and to perceive and to learn. Our Body is that greatest mystery of all, the Word made flesh. The Body and its health are deeply connected with Spirit and Soul. The task of education is to mature and to integrate these three realms, so that we may be ever more in harmony with ourselves and with our destinies on Earth.

Now, of course, there are other factors which work also within our wholeness and which make education dynamic and challenging. One is the fact that the human being grows and changes through many stages of development. Our bodies change drastically from early childhood to young adulthood and the older years. Our perceptions change, our feelings change, our ways of learning change. So our wholeness contains a lifeline of unfolding inner and outer forms and rhythms. Education must therefore be sensitive to what is happening *to whom and when*. In other words, we are called upon to understand what is right for a person at a particular time. There is much to be observed here, and more and more fully researched and understood through intuitive observation and imaginative perception. We need to be able to tell one *quality* of pleasure from another, one *quality* of suffering from another. We need to develop an ability to see how forms of growth unfold *from the inside out*. And we need to see how much growth comes through relationship with others—with our classmates and our teachers. And here we may need to think about some ways of fostering dependable human relationships during our schooling in the elementary and secondary grades.

One way, which has worked out well in certain schools, is to select teachers who will stay with their class, ideally, through all six or even eight grades.[1] They will not do all the teaching, but they will give the main lesson every morning, and will accompany the children like faithful friends through these growing years. Other lessons in specific daily practice, like foreign languages, handcrafts, outdoor work, and sports, will be shared by other faculty. It can be observed, in the schools where this happens, that

---

1. For example, the Waldorf Schools, begun in 1919 by Rudolf Steiner in Stuttgart, Germany, for the children of the workers in the Waldorf Astoria cigarette factory, and spreading now around the globe. This was also part of the advantage of the original model of the one-room schoolhouse and of the personal tutor to the advantaged children in the old days—the maintaining of a long and developing friendship.

the dynamic advantage to both teacher and student greatly out-weighs any imagined disadvantage.

The teacher, in such a situation, also grows from year to year, not repeating the same syllabus. We must begin to emphasize wholeness as an aspect of teachers as well as of children. It is the teacher's wholeness which must be equally our concern; the teacher's well-being of body, soul, and spirit. The neglect of the inner life of the teacher, in university training and in the ordinary school day, is, perhaps, one of the root causes for present day difficulties in the schools. The discontent and violence of students may well be an expression of their unwillingness to adopt the culture of their teachers, which may seem to them instinctively to be less than a satisfying life. They are unwilling to be governed by that model.

Teachers, because of the way they are trained, tend to think that their job is to offer their students subject matter, skills, and discipline. These are a desert, and fill the soul with hopelessness if they are not, at the same time, partners to wonder, enlightenment, imagination, drama, and the awakening of conscience and compassion—of creative response. To study nature without revering nature dries us up. We begin to think that our role on Earth is to control, to manipulate, to use, to exploit to our advantage. This doesn't work, as we are seeing. It bears poisonous fruits. And the reason it does not work is that it does not start from a ground of wholeness. It leaves out the necessary dialogue between the living Earth and the living person—their mutuality as features of divine presence. American Indians still retain a heritage of ancient spiritual Earth-knowledge. Perhaps they will turn out to be among our teachers in approaching a wholistic (i.e., holy) relationship to other two-leggeds and to four-leggeds, to trees and streams and oceans and mountains and, God willing, to the soil itself. Perhaps they will be able, as our hosts on this continent, to help us watch what we put in our air and water, and in our mouths and ears and noses and eyes. All these, they know, are powerful agencies.

A New Birth of Consciousness

We are living in an exciting and wonderful time of a birth of consciousness. We have had a long period, some 500 years, of developing capabilities of objectivity and independence in our thinking and observing. We call them Natural Science. We have experienced historically an earlier period when we lived the bidding of the gods. Now we wake to take on truth in inner freedom, finding our experience of Spiritual Presence each in our own way, each treading a ray of that inner Sun, tracing our own orbit through it. The human being is waking up in a new day of our journey toward a creative humanity we do not yet fully possess. We go to school as part of that quest.

So we may see the questions and difficulties of the time in which we live as signs and portents of the Genius of the Age at work. We may see that we are being called as a seed is called, to awake out of passivity—to become inwardly active, outwardly energized, creative in shared growth. And this surely is how we may read the meaning of those movements called "activism," "ecology," "rise of the arts and crafts," "community building."

Surely the presence of this essay, in its effort to share in the activity of living and learning toward wholeness, is itself a symptom of what is coming to life in our depths. If we hew to an image of an ongoing evolutionary continuum, a spiritual lifeline, like a Vine growing above ground and rooting below the surface, we may be able to get a feeling for the different seasons of growth.

In other words, there is no tone of reproach or of negativity in our meditations on the themes of our concern. We are not doing nor have we done things wrong. Rather, we are encouraged to be mindful that we live continually in a kind of questioning, an alert observing, so that when matters get out of tune, we can adapt to new needs and new conditions, quickening new capabilities. This is one of the ways that makes life so interesting and such an endless adventure and challenge. The reason that things get out of tune is that what may have been appropriate at one stage of development, or at one historical moment, is not supposed to be carved permanently in stone if it is to carry the lifeline. The lifeline is alive and continually forming and reforming and transforming. Even as it lasts, it changes, and corrects itself to stay on course.

When something that was good at one time is allowed to perpetuate itself longer than it should, it becomes toxic. For example, little children have a genius for learning by imitation, which is largely unconscious. For this reason, their surroundings of people and circumstances are their teachers. They literally drink them in. Their joy is to "play" house, "play" school, "play" doctor. In the adult, this kind of imitation of popular culture is imprisoning. We, as adults, want to know consciously how we feel about what is going on around us. We want also to create culture, to make new, to examine the values which are "given," and to work with them like a yeast, letting them rise to consciousness so that we know what bread we are eating. If we look at our ongoing lives in an imagery of the transformations which are called for, we do not then need to fear change or be threatened by it, but to realize that in fact we are creatures in whom change and growth and transformation are natural tendencies and talents. It is only when we suppress these tendencies that stiffening and hardening begin, and we fear to break our bones if we should take a new step.

Metamorphosis does not jeopardize our safety. Our safety is jeopardized only by the extremes of rigidity on the one hand and of mindless expansion on the other. Two diseases characterizing our epoch are arthritis, a hardening tendency, and cancer, a growth syndrome heedless of consequences.

Importance of Inner Pictures

Perhaps here another exercise for the imagination may become our meditation. For the pictures we hold in our minds of how life works, of what the human being is, of how things are held together—these inner pictures, which are usually what we mean when we refer to "the ideas we have about things"—are crucial. We want them to be accurate. We don't want to be duped either by wishful thinking or by fashionable pessimism and skepticism. We want the wholeness of life to give us the picture, and not to invent one by our own desire or ignorance. St. Paul mentions a time when we put aside childish things and see "face to face." In our century we want to know the facts. A sense of fact would be as worthy an aim for education as for the poet, as T.S. Eliot describes in his essay, "The Function of Criticism." The facts are of a cosmology and a theology, an outer world and an inner world, right down to how earthworms know how to digest and transform the Earth itself by an inner process. Neurophysiologists say it isn't possible to talk about neurons without talking about mind and body at the same time. The ideas we have, they say, affect our tissues.

Well, then, ideas, or pictures, count. They matter. The imagination matters. It is an organ by which we may perceive inner pictures which are expressed by physical matter and processes. You may wonder why I call Imagination an organ. Well, it is. It is a Sense Organ, which perceives meaning, by which Life Makes Sense! Meaning is found through the inner pictures we have of what life is all about. These pictures may be visual, or musical, or kinetic (inner movement), or spatial. They may have the feel of a contour of meaning which is not exactly sensory, but somehow beyond the senses. Let us call it meta-sensory or para-sensory, supersensory. That is, it is an inner experience, and yet, it is strong and tangible— like love. It is helpful to consider the possibility that Imagination, Inspiration, and Intuition are supersensory organs—spiritual organs. The reason why these inner pictures give us a sense of meaning is that we feel connected through them to life. Imagination, Inspiration, Intuition, perceive across the threshold. To feel that our lives are meaningful is to feel that our inwardness is connected with a spiritual world across the threshold of the senses. The senses are the portal. They are the hinge. There is no physical experience which is not a spiritual experience as well.

We feel ourselves to be part of a common task: to develop a humanity we do not yet possess, to keep the connection strong between our own interiority and the inwardness of others and of the universe, to know that what we think and feel and do affects the "facts of life," to feel the foundation of the new building of humanity deepen in our own resolve and rise in our imaginations, and to learn to practice what we preach. It sometimes seems that the real problem in our time is the Will. How do we get our bodies to carry out our compassion in deeds? This is the $64,000 question, isn't it! This is the question addressed by the sages and initiates of old. Buddha tried to get at an answering through the eightfold path. Jesus tried to get to an answering through parable and prayer. If it were easy, we would be farther along than we are. Since it isn't easy, and it isn't given, we go to school.

The Images in Words

Before turning to inner pictures, let us look first at what the word "school" means. Words carry primal insights. They too have evolved, and shed light on the history of consciousness. "In the beginning was the Word," marks the very start of St. John's gospel. In the beginning, words referred to concrete processes, things, relations. They have only lately become abstract. For example, our word *idea*, which comes from the Greek *eidos*, meant originally "a form." And *art*, which today means heaven knows what, comes from an ancient root, "to join." So does *religion*, from roots which mean "to bind together again, to be concerned." And *to know*, in the Bible, means to unite with in the flesh. So, if we are concerned about connections between science, art, and religion, we can notice that they are joined at the root.

But about *school* and *schooling*: here the root image is "a pause." This explains the popular association between school and leisure (see your closest dictionary). But we may "pause" (i.e., "school" ourselves) and reflect upon the image of pausing. When we pause, we inhibit automatic behavior. Behavior may be automatic in a variety of ways: it may be habitual, instinctual, compulsive, dogmatic, fearful, greedy, unconscious, eager, conditioned—and probably even a lot more ways than those. Automatic behavior is not bad or good. It depends. School, because it asks us to pause, gives us the opportunity to direct our behavior more deliberately. What has been automatic may now be chosen, or it may be reconsidered and revised. School, from this perspective, is like a musical rest. It offers a chance to breathe, to listen, to collect oneself, to come into relationship with what is going on around us, to take hold in a new way, or to let something go. Some partings may be "such sweet sorrow," as Juliet says, but some may also be like opening a window and letting in fresh air.

Life as a Playing Field

Pain is often associated with change because habits are strong in our flesh. To change our habits, we have to change our bodily patterns of response. Pain is also connected with consciousness. For example, we are only conscious of our stomachs when they ache. Becoming conscious of the need for change may cause pain. But that's okay. Pain is no enemy, no matter what the drug companies say. If we think of life as a playing field where we are to become emotional athletes, able to do what we need to do in a common human effort of building new forms when they are needed, then we won't begrudge pain. Athletes expect pain from stretching in order to do their best.

Not only American, but other cultures, share a love of physical sports and admire the disciplines they demand. We love to practice our jogging, our tennis, our bowling, our yoga, our t'ai chi, our gymnastics, handball, swimming, hiking, skiing, horseback riding, skating, surfing. How would it be if we would take up, in an imaginative meditation, the possibility of regarding our relationship to life as a kind of athleticism! How would it be if we would consciously practice, once a day, for six months, the change of a habit. For example, our handwriting! If we tend to write large with flourishes, to write small and regularly. If we tend to write in a small neat hand, to expand the size to twice or three times the height and width of the letters. The purpose would be to feel the possibility of freedom begin to infuse an automatic activity. A secondary purpose would be to experience writing as a sensory practice—a kind of drawing. For one of the powers working against our freedom and our imagination for inner growth and transformation is the mechanization of writing and other communication arts. If we are to be faithful to the picture of human wholeness, we must be careful to keep our values human rather than mechanical. The question should be not only what can a machine do, but also what shall human beings do. Our society invests more in machines than in persons. As a result, persons may have little to do, while the machines gulp fuel and whirr on. What is it really that we worship? What are the values implicit in our institutions and social behavior?

The pictures which give us strength and truth to live by come from a wholeness of life and its forms. They avoid a one-sided view, either of life's difficulties or of life's magnificence. How do we make sense of, how do we school ourselves, for the experience of so much good and so much evil, so much suffering and so much joy, so much fat and so much lean? How do we learn both acceptance and creativity? How do we live in paradox? For life is indeed beyond our logical comprehension, and yet totally within our Being. We are born from deep within its mystery; we know all about it somewhere in our blood and in our bones. Our heads may feel baffled, but our human wisdom surfaces again and again, in times of crisis, adversity, awe. When the lights go off in a big city, when there is a power breakdown, strangers befriend one another, take initiative in public confusion, are helpful and brave.

In wartimes, the most drastic and irreversible sacrifices are made. In times of public grief and mourning—or times of awe—greatness of spirit shines through. Though we fear death, we bear it. Deep life-wisdoms sustain us, all the while we are wringing our hands. The human being is a paradox: weak in some ways, strong in others; wise in some ways, foolish in others; mature in some ways, childish in others. This should make us both humble and hopeful, aware of our relative strengths, aware of our need for each other. The dynamic of opposites generates growth, when they are embraced by a wise and loving spirit. In a schooling for wholeness, lifelong, we may learn ever more to feel in ourselves this possibility: that the spirit within us is not divisive, but contains our inner contradictions like a vessel, that they may be reconciled and changed.

Crisis and Encounter

The views expressed here have been hard won, through crisis in my own long relationship to schools. Like most others, I was educated to be an intellectual of the verbal type. In the middle of life, I learned that knowledge did not make us wise or loving. Our education had been built upon the supremacy of cognitive skills: reading, writing, math, history, science, language, philosophy, culture. I became a college teacher of English, and before long found myself questioning the assumptions on which learning appeared to be based: namely, that the purpose of life is to be happy, to achieve status, and to make money; to be attractive, to satisfy our appetites, to be secure, and to win out over the other person. These did not jibe with my dreams for myself or the world.

In reaction against the imaginative flimsiness of the cognitive fabric, I turned to the arts, to handcrafts, and to community. There, at the other end of the stick, surely the answer would be found to my dream of human potential. Again, through crisis, I learned that making beautiful things does not in itself guarantee human values. And group endeavor, without sustained commitment by each member, ends in schism.

The assumptions on which my education was based fell into deep question. Neither the intellectual virtues, nor artistic talent, nor democratic organization could sustain life. What more is needed?

For several years I foreswore contact with schools and their clichés. I was fed up with the pretensions of knowledge, beauty, and togetherness. I had built my house upon them, and the floods had washed my house away, for it was built upon sand.

Where was the rock to be found? Where is the rock to be found, which will reunite knowledge, art, and human community as one entity, so that from this root may grow truth, beauty, and goodness? In the Middle Ages, the alchemists searched also for this transforming agent. They called it "The Philosopher's Stone." And it was to turn base metals into gold—not the gold of this world, they said, but a spiritual gold, incorruptible, imperishable. The process of transformation always started with the primal materials of existence: red dirt, dung, lead; with our common clay, our given nature. Within these the seeds of gold lie hidden. The Stone accelerates the process of their growth. It too is a paradox: as soft as wax, as hard as diamond. That is, it can be melted down again and again, and never lose its permanence, its sparkle. Various arts of transformation reflect this archetypal process. Through the ability to change, we manifest living form. In the crisis of my own life, I turned to pottery, the art of clay and fire. The parables of plasticity and ordeal by fire, of sacrifice and fruition, are spoken through its mouth implicitly. My troubled heart slowly grew quiet as my thinking and my feeling and my doing were refashioned—not through logic alone, but through participation in living, formative process. The hand and the clay were in dialogue. What were they? What is the human hand, what is clay? And what were they making together?

92

And why was the fire needed? And if the pot broke, what was left? Ah, so much to harken to. The Stone had been laid on the tomb of assumptions that needed to change. And a new quality of human wholeness rose from the pause. Nothing is wasted. Each step is on the way.

What we are called to surely is a Return to Source, a "turning" to the primal Rock from which the power of engendering springs. *Lord* in Greek is *Kyrie*. It means "Power," and turns easily in its sound to *Kirk* and to *Church*. We are called to build our power— i.e., our lord, our *kyrie*, our church, as inner capacities—upon rock, and to know that that rock is the gold of our inner person, its incorruptibility. Our inner person is part of the inwardness of the universe. It is divine presence in our bit of being. When we remember our connection, we are mindful of ourselves in our true nature. In us dwell the behemoth and the leviathan, the apple and the garden. We may choose to move toward maturity of consciousness, of responsibility, of forgiveness. We will find that the Garden of childhood changes as we journey on. Its landscape takes form as the vessel does, in mutuality of human hand and earthly clay. In each bit of being, the wholeness shines. Schooling may foster this alchemical image.

To Feel the Whole in Every Part

To feel the whole in every part: this picture of person and world-existence was given to me by working as a potter with clay on the potter's wheel. That the whole lives in every part is an ancient understanding, usually described in the relationship between Macrocosm (the big universe out there) and Microcosm (the universe repeated, in small, in us). Throughout history, in many cultures, there have been references to this law, this morphology. And it is finding contemporary expression in the hologram. It appears therefore to be part of Source, of primal connection between this side and that side, between "in here" and "out there." In our day we intend to question this primal connection until we can feel it afresh in ourselves. This is not an age of taking things on someone else's authority. It is a time of entering into our own authentic participation from a free base: entering through A Door which carries our figure as the shape of its opening. And thus do we suffer doubt and bewilderment, estrangement and despair, loneliness and fear, as we make the journey from a spiritual childhood, in which we were told everything which we were to believe, to a spiritual freedom in which we have free access to that Sun which radiates in all our different directions. Our Sun organ, our solar plexus, wakes to its Friend and Counterpart, when the time comes and we are ready. We cannot settle for less. We cannot settle for a security which is not right for our time, a security of sectarianism. It won't work. Boundaries must be softened and made transparent to the light. We must enter the evolving paradox of wholeness and of individuality. We are each distinct in our uniqueness and each a part of a common body. We do not know ourselves until we know this double nature. We do not know another person until we know our differences and the connections we share. We go to school to learn how to prepare ourselves to experience this double nature as a Oneness, a Fact. Therefore, the way we learn arithmetic must be from the sum to the parts. Remember the image of the heart as an organ that has two chambers. It won't beat or circulate the golden blood without this inner form. Similarly we will not live in warmth and feeling without a sense of our inner form: of an individual ego and a Higher Ego in Whom all persons share. In the Higher Ego of humanity we find the communion of humankind. We feel in ourselves this Quality of Being who knows that suffering is part of the journey to renewal, that education isn't always pleasant. Joy in truthfulness may make even of suffering a Sun.

When potters work on a potter's wheel, they throw a ball of clay in the center of the wheelhead, and make the wheel spin, either by kicking a fly wheel, which is connected to the wheelhead by a vertical axle, or by turning a switch. We wet our hands, and press the turning clay, up into a cone, down into a plane. Thus, we work the clay in opposite directions, narrowing and widening, as a single rhythmic movement, helping it to move into a condition of equilibrium. This process is called "centering." It is a way of assimilating all the molecules of the clay, all the variations of wetness and plasticity, to one another in an even grain. Each quality is distinct, yet each permeates the mass. Eventually, when centered, the clay resembles an unwobbling pivot. Then it can be opened with the fingers and formed into a vessel without falling apart. We take all the clay into our hands, and feel how the elements are integrating as we move. This process has to be repeated over and over again. It is not a matter of doing it once at the beginning and then forgetting about it. The clay continually goes off center as tensions arise; it is continually brought over and over again into center. Centering is a continuing activity; it is not a fixed condition. It is the discipline of bringing in rather than leaving out. It creates a vessel which can contain; can embrace; can be filled with light, emptiness, space, food, dirt, what you will. Once the ball of clay is in balance, fingers press into it gently, firmly, opening it into a cylinder. They raise the walls by pressing and lifting at just one point, through which the whole form passes. The belly swells out, the neck curves in, the rim bends. Whatever pressure we exert at one point forms the whole. Wherever we touch life, we form it. The whole of the cosmos is passing through our lungs, our bloodstream, our fingers, senses, soul, and spirit. Wherever we feel it, we form it. Do not forget the parable of the mustard seed, the power of the small.

We may carry in our soul this picture of creating little by little the vessel of our humanity. We may feel in any act the wholeness of ourselves and our warmth and our concern and our goodwill and our limitations, and we may know ourselves, therefore, in our hope and our imperfection. Knowing our humanity, we may be led by hope and imperfection to humility, good humor, mercy, and continual striving. We may experience this striving as a gentle movement, a flow of energy, to which we are alert and which we can to some degree guide into form. We try not to think of ourselves as bigger than we are, but to get a feel of "how much clay there is," and how we may little by little open it and stretch it and form it in an art of self-creation. We may think of the mysteries of fire and water and air and earth, of warmth and awareness, shaping us and taking shape through our response, a human dialogue which is also a cosmic dialogue. How small we are, and yet.... One might say the same of an atom, a neuron, an electron, a particle of light—how small, and yet in each there is a hologram of the whole!

It is essential that we keep very clear in our picture the power of our hands as they touch and listen and rest and support. Among all the ingredients of our wholeness, the creative power of the individual hand is decisive. We must be willing to take on, in consciousness, the mystery of our creative power. We share the generative character of the nucleus. Whether we are passive or active, we shape the world around us. Centering as reciprocal dialogue is continuous. Since silence speaks as loudly as words, what are we saying? And now that we are being asked about education, what do we say? How do we begin to think about it?

Always we must remember that we are not being asked to solve the problems of education for all time. We are asking ourselves to make a personal approach to the question and to find where we are and where we need to go now. We will discover that our response will have that double level which we ourselves have in relation to the world. We will find common and ongoing truths and laws about human creatures and their prospects; and we will find distinct tasks evolving organically out of the soil of this period of history. I like the picture that Rudolf Steiner gives of this process of "deciding" what to do. He points out that decision is always implicit in the situation, like the form of the growing plant is implicit in the bulb. If we are in touch with the situation, we will see what it wants, if it is to unfold in a healthy way. Likewise, if we know children, we will know what they want to learn, and how, and what they hope for in their relationships to grown-ups, and how they wish to be (because they are) a part of history and the present and future—to know that they belong in the world. They are part of The Real Thing.

The Crossing Point

Another picture of "how things work and what life is really all about" may be found in the study of plant growth and projective geometry. That's where I came across it. Like centering, it is an archetypal picture, an imagination which reveals Source. We may find its law working in many other places. It is the law of the fusion of opposites: whether they be left brain/right brain; subject/object; inner/outer; dream/reality; night/day; sleeping/waking; death/life. The continuum, the form, is expressed by the wholeness which contains these opposites and breathes by their means. They may be compared to the two sides of a plane, or ribbon. The geometric form is called a lemniscate. *Lemnis* is the Latin word for "ribbon." A lemniscate is a figure eight made as a plane rather than as a line. It has two surfaces, like a Moebius strip. Its genius is that if you run your finger round the inside of the bottom loop and through the point where it crosses at the center of the 8, you will find your finger on the outside of the upper loop without ever having lifted it, and then again as you proceed around the outside of that loop and through the crossing point you will be on the inside, and so on.

We do not have to choose whether to be outward or inward, practical or visionary. We are both. It is our genius, as human creatures. Our feet are on the ground. Our heads are full of dreams, and we listen with an inner ear. We draw inspiration from an inner voice, and have intuitions of meaning and connection. We may tend more in one direction than another: more off earth, more down to earth. But we live in a crossing point, a simultaneity of

Earth and Heaven, sensory and supersensory. Part of our human task is to learn to balance that flow. Earthly life teaches us truths we could not learn without the experience of physical matter and sense perception. We could not learn aloneness, nor love, without the separate existence of our body. We could not learn freedom without separation. Through inner development, we may ourselves become star-like, inner Suns. Ultimately we are meant to illumine the heavens anew with human warmth and creative initiative mercy-filled. The relationship between inner development and cognition is the ground of education. We are cautioned to take three steps in moral development for every step we take in knowledge. How is this to be done? My hunch is that morality is a strong sense of connection, that it is built in, as are connections themselves, and that the moral imagination may be awakened as the sense of wholeness is awakened.

The form of the lemniscate is expressed with special charm in the plant world. Take any beet or radish or carrot. I select these because the difference between the bottom and top "loops" is so marked. But so would it be for that matter in a rose bush or dandelion. The plant, when it germinates, grows in two directions: down and up, root and shoot. The layer out of which these directions differentiate is called The Crossing Point, and it is sometimes only one cell wide (the power of the small!). As the plant matures, the gesture of the root as it digs into the dark earth is very different from the growth above ground in the sunlight. The root tends to be convex, bulbous, fleshy around the solid core. The leaves and flowers tend to extend in planes around a hollow center. The plant grows by opposite energies. It contracts into a stem, expands into a leaf, contracts into a bud, expands into a flower, contracts into a seed. And what is this seedpoint but a teensy capsule of invisible formative forces in the guise of a speck of cellulose? Genetic material, they call it. What is material about it? A seed certainly doesn't look like much of anything, until you begin to see with a double eye, not only the outer husk but also the inner "void" of genesis. See how important it is, what fun it is, not to say what a seed is, or life is, but to live in the question, opening it, like a Door, like a Christmas present, opening it up, noticing, noticing, all the time; seeing not only with the organ eye but with the inner eye as well.

Perhaps it is the education of this inner eye that we should speak about next.

If, as the picture tells us, the form of the flower lies somehow implicit within the bulb, and it is a question of providing proper conditions for growth, then we may think of education as providing conditions for growth. We surround the person with what is suitable for the unfolding growth of its threefold being. Already we are in a question: what is growth? For we can see that a plant may in a certain sense "grow" no matter what. In one soil it will be tall and spindly; in another, short and bushy. In one season it may bloom, in another not. Growth, then, is a formative process. There is such a thing as desirable growth and not so desirable growth. In the human being, growth occurs not only in the physical body, but in our emotional development, in our cognitive development, in our social development, our creative development. If we stay with our picture of the human being as threefold, body-soul-spirit, living in outer behavior and inner meaning simultaneously, we will see that growth is no simple matter. It can easily get out of whack: too much of one thing, not enough of another; too much stalk, not enough flower; too much flower and not enough leaf (like when my lettuce bolts early). Part of the teachers' art is to watch the balanced growth of their pupils. And they are helped in this by the picture of the person as an artistic, creative, knowing, learning, feeling creature, growing from a single root. One root, many branches. In this sense, what we do in physical education affects our emotional development, and vice versa. How we develop our feeling will affect how we learn and what we learn. Emotional conditions for learning are fundamental. There are things we simply cannot perceive unless we open ourselves to receive the world with reverence.

How Children Learn

With a little child, the learning is primarily imitative, brilliantly so: learning to speak, to do chores, to relate socially, to handle materials, to sing, to play, to paint, to care for animals and plants, to care for others. These will be most likely to "grow" where the environment provides vital models, friends in the process. The way adults speak, the things they laugh at, how they eat and drink and smoke, the way they move, all this is "teaching" the children. Children are like wondrous sense organs, imbibing the world around. How they experience what they take in is a matter of individual temperament and destiny.

It is a concern of teaching to observe temperament, to work with it, to help it to grow toward balance, to use its particular talent well. In every class, the choleric child, the sanguine child, the phlegmatic child, the melancholic child has its part to play, its offering to make. For there is not only our personal wholeness to ponder on, but the human family, made up, as it is, of all our different flavors. To honor the different flavors is part of early schooling. Through stories and examples, a mood may be created in which every little person knows she or he has a gift for the world. In the community of a class and a school, there must from the beginning be a spirit of respect for different gifts and abilities. There should be no grading nor failing, no mockery nor sarcasm. The teacher, like a parent, should carry the children along affectionately and faithfully.

Evaluations are made, of course; and reports should be shared with parents—but not in terms of social failure, or precocity. The kind of intelligence we want to encourage is a central question. What spirit do we want our intelligence to have? Do we want children to be gifted and alienated? Literate and prejudiced? Brilliant and cynical? Intelligent and materialistic? In need of help and ashamed? Right here we must be most disciplined in keeping faith with wholeness. Unless we educate for wholeness in person

100

and wholeness of our Earth planet, we are not really intelligent. In our school subjects, we have an opportunity to study humankind as a family, and the Earth as the body of that family. We have the possibility of developing a curriculum which is like a map of its dreams and its history, a map of interconnections. Interdisciplinary methods try to avoid squeezing the life out of one part and blowing it up in another. The health and wholeness of our planet is not separable from the health and wholeness of us as individuals. We are part of it all. We cannot escape the karma of our time. We see, everywhere, evidence of what happens when the law of wholeness is transgressed: war, poverty, bloated affluence, bloated hunger, injustice, despair, guilt, poisoned food, poisoned air, poisoned water, greed, and indifference. "What shall we do?" we ask. We shall begin from a new point and proceed to a different end. We shall begin with a concern for wholeness and proceed to an education, lifelong, which serves this in spirit and in practice.

Special Children

Some children are in need of special soul-care: the retarded and mentally handicapped through autism, aphasia, hydrocephalus, cerebral palsy, Down's syndrome, and other afflictions. Particularly, here, one must transform the conventional standards of intelligence and worth. The social offering to be made by these children, in addition to their special modes of perception, is significant. They often live much closer to Source than the rest of us. And their relationship to hardship, disappointment, frustration, and social embarrassment is deeply instructive to those who consider themselves normal. The handicapped awaken a sense of human grace, body-free. They reconnect us with unconditional love and open our eyes to particularities of form. Often, in their freedom from conventional patterns of social adaptation, they show themselves to be open to growth where others stumble. I am thinking particularly of their capacity for helping one another and for community spirit, in addition to their aptitudes in the care of animals and of the land, and in artistic expression and the crafts. To behold self-respect in those who by popular standards are neither attractive nor smart nor able to manage by themselves, is to behold a revelation. Questions of their education are ongoing. But one thing is sure, and that is their contribution to human community. They slow us down. They give us pause. Part of our schooling is to receive them and to feel in ourselves the awakening of new capacities for mutuality. What is more important to learn?

Elementary School

We have said that the inner will of the child responds to early environment, each in its own way. By the time of elementary school and the change of teeth, inner changes take place as well: increased interest in drama, vulnerability to mood, curiosity about how things work, growing selfhood and independence, peer love, and a genuine friendship with adults who can be trusted. Friendship with a trustworthy adult seems especially fruitful during the years 7-14. The teacher in school, with luck, can be such an abiding friend, who does not trick nor deceive nor abandon. It is this quality of authority which young children enjoy and learn from. The trusted adult's relationship to learning and knowing may be the child's inspiration. For this reason, a materialistic view of the class teacher as nothing more than an information bureau and a police officer is devastating. For the children, the spirit of their teacher shapes their inner organs. Thought of in this way, children's painful outbursts are more understandable.

In the tiny child, it is the sleeping Will which is the vital energy, radiating through all other facets. In the child between 7 and 14, it tends to be the dreaming Feeling. If the Will has been given expression, it tends to transform into increasingly socialized feeling. And the physical growth forces, having completed much of their work in building the body and its organs, metamorphose into forces of imagination and inner growth, as areas of individual feeling begin to mature. The education of the elementary school years should be based on imagination and feeling as a stage in the development of intelligence and wholeness. The studies in the curriculum should be presented by the teachers with personal enthusiasm, and in imaginative ways which give the children pleasure and challenge them to work. With children, often their keenest pleasure comes from work well done.

From the beginning of school, artistic expression should infuse cognitive learning. Colored pencils and crayons should not be restricted to an hour of art each week (as is often the case in public schools), but should be used as a matter of course in all lessons, such as arithmetic, writing, social studies, biology. Pupils should make their class books and decorate them with drawings. They should express their feelings in poems and pictures and collage. Information should always keep its connection with life rhythms and imaginative examples, enabling the children to continue their inner picturing in relation to what they are learning. Bodily activity in relation to numbers and letters and speech and music can be a part of daily practice right from the beginning, as well as specific instruction in gymnastics and dance. Working in the arts—singing, playing an instrument, knitting, crocheting, sewing, embroidery, modeling, carving, woodworking, dramatic acting—should insure the balance of the days. The direction is toward the child's growing wholeness.

Another element in these years, to be considered from the point of view of educating the whole person, is to remember that the human person is both individual and collective in nature. Physically, we recapitulate in the womb the evolution of our species. Psychologically, we recapitulate, during the years of schooling, the evolution of consciousness. The mind of the six-year-old, in that archetypal sense which we mentioned earlier, is not the same as that of a twelve-year-old or an eighteen-year-old or a forty-year-old. The child-psyche is still undifferentiated and corresponds to a kind of mythic consciousness. The curriculum of the elementary years might well correspond to the gradual coming to birth of modern consciousness, which could be symbolized by the stage of puberty, the birth of the young adult.

The curriculum therefore should nourish an inner development which accompanies changes in physical development. We may begin with myths and fairy stories, telling them aloud, asking the children to tell them aloud—dramatizing and acting out—using their voices, naturally and lustily, in telling and talking and singing. Yes, my goodness, yes, the question of children's voices: how veiled and faltering they often sound in school—false in the presence of feared adults—or strident and antagonistic. Why does human speaking fare so badly in our public schools?

Puberty and High School

At puberty there occur dramatic physical changes. Limbs shoot out, jaws develop, voices mature, sexuality becomes more powerful. These are both individualizing and generic. At the same time, a capacity for more abstract thinking is enlivened. A strong idealism, as well as argumentativeness, emerge. A new emotionalism and sense of aloneness flood the youth's being. In high school there is a greater penetration into the phenomenal world, keeping the artistic and feelingful and social integrated with cognitive development. During these years, there should be more attention given to practical work, vocational service, community participation. Craftsmanship, technology, musicianship, farming and gardening, shoemaking, cooking and baking, tailoring, architecture (building and carpentry, design), landscaping, geologic research, surveying, boat-building and sailing—we can't list them all. The point is that during the high school years there must be practical work activity, as well as further intellectual training and artistic creativity. When one works practically, intelligently, and creatively, in any given task, one is working with wholeness. And the kind of practicality, intelligence, and creativity we are talking about remains always faithful to person-as-spirit-being on a living Earth with fellow persons with whom we are intrinsically connected, in an ecology of human being and nature. What is divisive is not practical, intelligent, nor creative. What is short-sighted and self-serving is not practical, intelligent, or creative in the long run. If this sounds like preaching, it is based on hard facts. The world we have built on money, speculation, greed, and competition is volatile and unstable. Because it is not grounded in a commitment to Person and Wholeness, it is inefficient and dangerous. Evil, someone has said, occurs when we are out of touch with our deepest being.

If these images of high school education seem different from the usual college preparatory pattern and, therefore, likely to put the later career of the youth in jeopardy, they are meant to be prophetic of steps toward a new culture in higher education as well. Adult education is in similar crisis and needs re-visioning from a wholistic view of the human being right for our time. As consciousness develops and our values grow and change, these will be reflected in education and society. For it is with this riddle that our inquiry began: why is it if we are all so bright and well-educated that the world is in such a mess? We began to try to look more consciously at the unconscious assumptions of our schooling, and to cast some new directions.

What Can We Do?

What can we do, who are neither children in the schools nor their teachers, to help to transform and guide education in a more wholistic and, therefore, more healthful direction? We must, of course, be "concerned." That is to say, we must live the religious life. We must feel wholeheartedly the inner will "to bind together again." This is the meaning of "religion." We must be willing to suffer the dynamics of questioning and correcting, and to be patient with our efforts so long as their direction is sustained and does not "wobble" too much. We may then live with children, whenever we are with them, in a condition of inner schooling: a sensitivity to our mutual uniqueness and mystery and participation in divine being; a sensitivity to what is appropriate to different ages, trying not to treat children as if they are miniature adults. Perhaps the difficulty comes because, though we are large and grown up, we are emotionally childish. And so we imagine that children are not so different from ourselves. But when we are a child of seven, we are different than when we are a child of forty-seven. We must become more aware of these things.

At home we may endeavor to be that friend and "authority" whom the child's soul wishes to depend on and be cherished by. As we offer our own self-respect, we feed the child's imagination for his and her own emerging maturity.

We may also meet together, parents and friends and teachers, to talk about our ideals and questions in goodwill. Teachers need support from the public for their own creativity and enthusiasm and growth. Teachers are rarely encouraged to grow and change. They are expected to keep on doing what they were hired to do. Reiteration is taken for dependability. The lives and education of teachers may be the most crucial question of all. It may be that they suffer more from spiritual neglect than any other group in education. Perhaps it is the adults we should be most concerned for.

It may be partly a question of the kind of picture we have of what an adult is. If our model is youth-centered, with the years of growth and creative vitality climaxing at about thirty, with a steady plateau and eventual downhill after that, no wonder we secretly long to remain childish. Who could love an adult, or want to be one? We need to awaken an inner picture of the dynamic soul life of adults, the stages of development as they continue from twenty-eight onward—the transformations, revelations, deepenings, increase of selfhood and the juiciness of experience, ripeness of humor and warmth, courage tested by adversity, change of direction and broadening of interests and skills; growth of tolerance and compassion and gentleness and an ability more and more to pause, to reflect, to laugh heartily, to live in the crossing point of inwardness and outwardness. In the early years, social adaptation is important: learning a skill, getting a job, a mate, a family, a neighborhood, a career, a personal life. Gradually these turn into other concerns, and at last a gradual preparation for the total inwardness of death. It is inspiring to grow up into adulthood, and to feel one's perceptions become more just, more generous, less biased—to feel in touch with a spiritual continuum so firm and mobile under one's feet.

The education of the whole person applies to us all: children, teachers, friends, and parents. It is a common question and striving.

Summary

Let us look back now at the journey we have come together in these pages. We have started with the question: What about the public school and the education of the whole person? We have entered the question as an inner realm which we may explore. We have called it a temple, and our explorations are a listening and a seeking. We find that an answering vibrates in the air. This is our first step. Already it tells us that our school and person are expressed both outwardly and inwardly. We find that what has brought education to crisis is a loss of meaning, a loss of respect, a fading sense of connection. We begin to see that these are symptoms of a search for health, for wholeness. Illness is a function of our health. The old ways are dying so that new forms can arise. It is a time of birth in consciousness. We feel an excitement in the air as we enter into the adventure of renewal. Change is painful for old habits. But pain is often the consequence of opening ourselves and stretching for new tasks. We turn from the temple to the playing field, and take on the discipline of imaginative athleticism.

We see that imagination gives us pictures of life, like an inner sense organ, perceiving meaning. We know that the ideas we have affect our bodies. So we look for pictures which are integrative, which accommodate the genius of the human being. We are creatures of paradox. We express both continuity and transformation, both practical survival and creative envisioning. We look to the images of centering and the crossing point, wholeness and individuality.

We find that words themselves, like *school, religion, art, to know*, give us insights into meaning and connections. If the popular assumptions on which education appears to be based are questioned, where do we turn for stability? Where is the rock to be found? It is to be found in the creative purposeful tendency in the spirit itself. It is to be found in the threefoldness of person and of society. It is to be found in a concern for wholeness of the Earth and in evolving individuality. Education must also seek to build on this rock.

How do the body, soul, and spirit of a child enter into the educational process? Changes in consciousness accompany bodily changes. Intelligence awakens first through imitation and will in the early years, then through feeling and imagination through the elementary years, and through a capacity for abstract thought based on living forms after puberty. The intelligence we want to encourage will be creative, practical, emotionally mature, lucid. The lucidity we look for, the objectivity we seek, is filled with reverence. Intellect without human warmth and without an intuitive sense of connection, of form, and of wholeness puts us in jeopardy. Education then must foster these capacities, which may serve to inspire steps toward a new culture.

Society too has its threefold aspect: economics, politics, cultural life. Each has its special teaching to offer: through economics we may learn to be fraternal; through politics we may learn to be just and to share rights equally with all; through culture we may learn to be free in spirit and to take initiative confident of its social function. These are the archetypal virtues of Liberty, Equality, Fraternity.

One question we have not asked is the relationship between money and education as work. Until our motivation to work is separated from money, we cannot move forward very far toward social renewal through the Door we have chosen. Wages should not be considered payment for work. We are not hirelings. Work is a right. Enough money to live so that we can continue to work is also a right. The bitterness of most social disputes comes from a distortion of the roles of money and work. Here, too, an answering is to be found within the temple: we go forth to do our work, and our needs are met by free gifts. Was this not the advice given to the disciples? It is also a foundation stone for building a threefold social order. The meaning of money is also to be explored. Its power derives from the ancient mystery of gold, of the Sun. Perhaps what we really long for is the divine gold sought by the alchemists: the gold of truth, beauty, and goodness. Money in the marketplace is its shadow.

Teachers in public schools have come to think of themselves as civil servants doing a job. This is too self-hurtful to bear. They are guides and models for the young. They are chiefs, teaching the boys and girls their heritage: how to hunt and gather, how to sow and harvest, how to read the weather, how to dance and worship, how to pray and wait, how to recite the poems and paint the legends, to walk the wilderness, to communicate with others far away.

Teachers' lives and destinies are as real and central to education as are children's. Care for their wholeness should begin in their professional training and should continue throughout their career. Since the vital practice of educational policy is in their hands, they should share in its formulation. For this they need opportunities to study and reflect together in a common commitment to inner growth.

It is customary to speak of academic *disciplines* in referring to a course of study. Part of the dilemma of education today may be a sign of this historical moment, when the disciplines of subject matter are being transformed by being interfused with the *disciplines of wholeness* based on a deep awareness of the total nature of the human being. The first discipline may be sincerity. Suffering in our society can begin with the duplicity of our schooling. We learn to mouth the language of idealism and freedom, and yet see it used as a mask for materialism and greed. Teachers need to rediscover their own hearts, to recover their own inner child, and to strengthen their courage for wholeness of soul. For they are always teaching by what they give off. Children too often learn cynicism as they learn their arithmetic. We are not economic animals. Soul hunger, our society shows us, is not quenched by affluence.

We need to take steps in two directions: inward and outward. The wholeness of the human being can furnish the methods of our schooling and our social goals. Like the flower in the bulb, the new forms are organically implicit in our evolving humanity and the larger spiritual world of which we are a part. The dependence of schools upon the shifting politics of government for their budgets and regulations deserves to be questioned. Nor should curriculum be determined by the textbook industry. Let teachers depend less upon textbooks and more upon their own inspiration and enthusiasm and selection of materials. For if teachers are not glad to go to school, why should children be?

The transformation of our schooling is part of the steady longing of our planet for self-completion. The economics and administration and content of schools are interconnected, not only locally, but in the deeper layers of stress and hope between countries. Though the territory of our concern is focused at HOME, HOME itself now feels the tensions of the globe. The education of the whole person represents a steady resolve to experience all the Earth and humanity as our Home, irradiated with a Spiritual Sun. Then all territories shall know themselves to be united in a warmth of commitment to one another. This commitment shall then be able to find its expression in a further evolving of an enlightened economics, administration, and content.

We must begin with a new consciousness of formative process and the vast interweaving of human life and social institutions. Wouldn't it be wonderful if our schools would decide to become learning centers for human and social renewal: cultural organs formed by teachers and parents uniting together to create living situations in which person and society can grow toward wholeness. The public school has a double role. It provides a continuity in the history of human consciousness, by transmitting culture and passing on skills. We stand on the shoulders of generations. And it is a place for engendering the new, the prophetic, the needed. As we have pictured the human being, we are both the products of history and the makers of history. Both historic humanity and prophetic humanity are the responsibility of education. Our hope is to awaken courage for change when it is needed. Change is part of life's continuity. It provides stability. Transformation is a natural aspect of growth. We give consistency to our lives by integrating the practical, creative, and moral aspects. Morality and a sense of meaning are joined at the root. They are built in, and need but to be awakened. Ours is a time of pioneering. There is so much exciting work to be done. The foundations of the new building of humankind are deepening in the spirit of our age, the contours are rising, the people are walking in. The vitality of youth and the inspiration of teachers and the imagination of parents and friends will help to create educational forms for public service. Remember the power of the small, the power of person. Remember that through Person sounds the Universe. Each of us can take a step toward wholeness in our own way. Together we can be co-creators of our age. We live in the threshold, at a frontier. Our meditation must always be upon the Door of Truth and of Life through which we enter.

Closing Hymn

Sweetness stores in the root,
sap rises and descends.
The rhythms of our nature
round us round.
Human Beings, risen,
take eternal life in hand.
Our creative light
shares in world creation.
The Life-Line of our Schooling
is its golden vein.

Supplementary Reading Suggestions:

Barfield, Owen. *History in English Words.* New York: Faber and Faber, 1943.

James, Charity. *Young Lives at Stake.* New York: Agathon Press, 1972.

——*Beyond Customs: An Educator's Journey.* New York: Agathon Press, 1973.

Richards, Mary Caroline. *Centering: In Pottery, Poetry, and the Person.* Middletown: Wesleyan University Press, 1964.

——*The Crossing Point.* Middletown: Wesleyan University Press, 1973.

——*Toward Wholeness: Rudolf Steiner Education in America.* Middletown: Wesleyan University Press, 1980.

Steiner, Rudolf. *The Kingdom of Childhood.* London: Rudolf Steiner Press, 1974.

——*The Roots of Education.* London: Rudolf Steiner Press, 1968.

After Wholeness,
What?

I have always been a person more comfortable with learning the arts of mediation than the arts of resistance. More persuaded of the need for reconciliation, seeing both sides of the question, than for a passionate priority. One is taught the values of unselfishness, humility, surrender, loyalty to the needs of the other. One is advised not to make waves, not to be contentious, not to make oneself conspicuous. One learns to be accommodating to experiences one would not have chosen: to be culturally cooperative, acculturated, keeping one's reservations and misgivings and self-dislike to oneself. Eventually, a kind of numbness takes over, masked often by an ironic humor. Real feeling seems crippled, difficult to arouse. Moral intuitions are stunted on behalf of social consensus. Conscience sleeps as we study detachment, objectivity, scientific rationality. An illusion of moral superiority covers the surface of our intellectualism. We have forsworn spontaneity, intuitive perception, emotional confidence, artistic independence, passionate grace.

And we have done all this purposefully, to develop certain soul powers, which must then be sacrificed for our next needed development. Some of us have been for the past fifty years working diligently to find our way to wholeness—integrating the shadow aspects of ourselves, learning to love the enemy, to dialogue with our unconscious. We have learned discrimination in order to love each thing, each being, equally. We have practiced opening ourselves to whatever comes. God has created all things that all things may flourish. This has been the discipline of what one may call the intellectual soul. It has been the path of human growth and development since, one might say, Pilate asked "What is truth?" and washed his hands of the matter.

We can say that truth is the Now, that's all there is. And we can also say that truth lives like a seed within life and develops slowly within human imagination. It seems to grow and to give hints of itself through paradox and polarity.

Our intellectual education has dried the soul as it did its work of developing objectivity and detachment, emotional restraint. Now we are learning that after each development, we must reintegrate with the rest of the body and being. Our emotions, our passions, are stunted and warped by having been carefully separated from moral intuitions, as we have conscientiously developed objectivity and unselfishness. To question unselfishness is to look more carefully at our sense of self. When we are unselfish, we are working against the primal devouring energy—we are imagining the good of the other before our own gratification. Gradually, our emotional patterns change, and we find ourselves less devouring and devoured. Then we may begin to give more loving attention to ourselves, feeling the self's hungers and potential, inviting the self to bring its light out from under the barrel and to shine. The self then is not a threat to our goodness—it has become a breathing of divine joy.

Now our task is to develop new organs of passion, grounded in the body which has learned deeply to perceive differences and to withhold judgment. Such a body responds to experience differently than one stressed by guilt, depression, and fear—prejudice and hatred.

After wholeness, what? The wholeness has been experienced. It has been centered in our very clay, our very substance, so to speak. Now may passions rise anew, clarified by the centering disciplines. Now may the heart speak its original poetry.

Persons evolve through stages of development. Centering and wholeness are one, but there are more to come. Persons continue to emerge, to be born ever more fully into existence.

There is a time for everything under the Sun, as the wise elder said: a time for grief and a time for joy, a time for selflessness and a time for fulfillment, a time for detachment and a time for passionate priorities, passionate grace!

A time for the philosopher and a time for the clown, until they marry and merge: God's fools, with a direct line to wisdom, humor, modesty, compassion, social justice, beauty, and the cosmic pratfall!

I have recently had an experience which has been a turning point. It is the awakening of the sensation of outrage, and in a way that has felt harmonious with the flow of life, nonviolent and active, giving me a sense of balance more like an acrobat or dancer than a weightlifter or judge. Not hostile nor as an adversary, but clear, affectionate, imaginative, generous, humorous. Ah! I think I could not trust the outrage if I had not required of myself the long practice of nondiscrimination, of inclusion, of sacrifice, the practices of wholeness, of centering.

Now for the story of my "radicalization."

I was invited to the campus of a western university in a large city. I was to participate in a curriculum conference, and to make presentations in local high schools and a community college. In my first meeting with sixty or so high school "honor students," I spoke first about artistic participation, and then I said I would show a few slides and asked for the lights to be turned off. They could not be turned off. A janitor and two engineers were hastily summoned. While they scratched around on the walls, I continued with my slides with the lights on. Then they were suddenly off. Good. I finished and asked for the lights to be turned on. They couldn't be turned on! The bell rang and the students groped their way out in the dark. I was left somewhat stunned as I had not been able to make my closing remarks to complete what

I had wanted to say. What had happened? The explanation was something about "a central computer." Obviously, control of the environment was no longer in the hands of human participants.

When that was over, I went to another class, at 10:30, to give a clay workshop. Several of the children were eating their lunches on the worktables—on trays from the cafeteria. What was to be done? Hurry them through their meal? Postpone the session? Chuck the food? I felt great concern for the young people who were trying to eat. They had obviously not been planned for. It all seemed hectic and uncaring, though full of goodwill with an upbeat young teacher. What are these children learning, I asked myself. They are certainly not learning to be sensitive to one another.

In the conference on the weekend, I noticed that there was no neutral place between air conditioning and heat—again the central computer was telling us we had to be hot or cold, under its control. The obsession with electricity was beginning to scare me. And our inability to say how we want to live. However, what tore the rag off the bush (an old southern saying) was discovering that the centerpiece of the buffet table in our catered coffee-hour was plastic flowers. I remember the moment well. It was excruciating. I saw the flower arrangement. I reached out to touch the petals. "They're not flowers," I howled in an anguished wail. "They're plastic!" Friends looked around dully (it seemed to me). Of course, they're plastic! Of course they're not real, they seemed to say. What's all this fuss about?

That's when outrage flared in my body and soul. I would not be content with falsity. I would not spend my life under the control of a central computer. I would try to rouse the senses of my professional colleagues and friends to find this make-believe life intolerable. What are the students learning? Not to be able to tell the real thing from a fake? Not to be able to tell the difference between a sound made in the air (the true medium of sound and of tone) and one reproduced by electricity?

116

The director of the conference asked for feedback in relation to the curriculum planning we had done. I said my feedback would consist of sending fresh flowers to his department every month and a painting I would create for his hallway, not by computer but by human touch. I have done both.

Later on, I had a dream in which the director of this conference and I are finding our way to "the new Earth." I hope we all are. The serious intent behind this feedback is to reeducate the senses. Hopefully, in due course, having had their habits changed to expect the real thing, the people will find falsity intolerable. The problem, of course, is that these are not the people who order the plastic centerpiece. My hope is that the consumers will gently remove the fake and replace it with what is beautiful and true. My hope is that we will become active on behalf of our real values.

It occurs to me that what has helped me is that I live in an agriculturally based community with mentally handicapped adults. There is very little abstraction in such a context. We tend to be surrounded by real things and creatures: cows and sheep and chickens and babies and grown-ups and fields and gardens and trees and plants and bushes and houses and cars and stoves and each other.

By the end of the week, I knew I had been "radicalized": new sensations and new behaviors had been birthed in me. I was returning home with a deeper commitment to the values of our little community and a readiness I had not had before to take extreme action. I was ready now, as I had not been before, to support our farmers' impulse to get rid of gas- and oil-consuming machinery and turn to farm horses for plowing and field work. I was ready to join a general strike against the nuclear reactors only ten miles from our front door by turning off my electric kilns, lights, radio, heater.

This process is, of course, a mysterious journey, a secret route for each one of us, from indifference to an energetic awakening, from not caring to caring, from numbness to passion, from fear to confidence, to grace. We cannot do it alone. We need angels to help us. That's for sure.

Imagination and Authenticity as Doorways to Creation

Plymouth Church, Oakland,
March 13, 1992

Imagination is spiritual perception. Authenticity is spiritual presence.

In reflecting on the theme of this talk, authenticity and imagination appeared in my inner eye, as companions. We can think of authenticity as the quality of expression, and imagination appears as the realm of Source, what authenticity draws upon. Or the other way round: authenticity gives us the impulse, imagination gives us the image. We need the courage of authenticity to carry the originality of imagination into expression. Whichever way you want to figure it, imagination and authenticity are the double-doors to creation. That's all pretty abstract, but it's an equation that excites me as it stands behind creative process.

Poem

Across the Golden Gate from San Francisco
Between the Bay and the Pacific
Lies Marin County.

When I was living
in Berkeley I would sometimes spend Sunday
Walking across the ridge above Muir Woods
Between Mill Valley and Stinson Beach.

Once
I walked washed there in empty air and heard
Between the ocean's grand oblivion and
The white stair of the city one small bird
Sing, all prodigal, to his bare theater.
Since,
He inhabits my mind high on a wire and
Wonders me what imagination means.

Imagination means singing to a wide invisible audience. It means receptivity to the creative unconscious, the macrocosmic mind, the artistic mind. It makes erotic philosophers of us, as we imagine the world in images that make whole. To imagine is to give birth to—to embody the spirit in Word and picture and behavior. The world will change when we can imagine it differently, and, like artists, do the work of creating new social forms.

BEHOLDING is also a way of imagining, and when heart and throat open, song arises as simple as breathing. Behold, as spring comes, "a god falling into life!"

Imagination is a bridge between our ordinary senses and the archetypal world which transcends the senses. It is the world of images which can inspire us, nourish us. It is also a world of daimonic powers that can harm us. We need to develop our authenticity, our inner I AM, to receive SOPHIA, our sacred Wisdom, to learn to guide our tiny craft through cosmic waters. The English Romantic poets said that Imagination was the capacity to experience what is absent as if it were present. Dreams, right? and hunches. Intuitions. Inspirations. Guides to the heart, where the heart is, the heart of the matter, what matters. What imagination means!

Authenticity is not a word you hear very often; it is not a word one uses very often. And yet I remember times when I have used that word to describe especially the work of children or of adult beginners. It seems to be connected with innocence and with guilelessness. It seems sincere, earnest, unselfconscious. Different observers would find it in different places. Authenticity means, first of all, a certain relation to oneself. It means a kind of willingness to be oneself, a courage and enthusiasm, perhaps quiet; it calls to mind always the real thing. In the dictionary, *authenticity* is defined as "genuineness," and the word *genuine*, it points out, contains an image of the knee. In French, *genou*, "knee," one bows the knee before the real thing.

Authenticity may seem bold, for it's often original, one of a kind. Separate from consensus. One comes to it through trust in one's own self, and a willingness to entrust oneself to others, whatever the risk. Vulnerability at some point dissolves into stillness. This stillness can act, and does act, for children and for the child in oneself, as a kind of buffer, an insulating protection, which allows one to be authentic and at risk in a natural way.

At one time I had a pottery studio to which the neighboring children would come to make things. On one memorable occasion, I was stacking the kiln—that is, I was putting things that we had made out of clay and had painted with glaze into the kiln where they would be fired to a high temperature. The glaze would melt and the piece that looked like a dusty gray now would emerge bright blue: wonderful. One child, Lisa, about nine years old, was bringing to me a small piece to be put into the kiln. It didn't look like anything in particular, just a kind of curved plane; maybe it was broken off of something else. But Lisa had glazed it carefully and was bringing it to me. "What's that, Lisa?" I said. "It's art," she said solemnly.

Obviously, I've never forgotten that moment. It was an epiphany, a revelation. From the mouths of babes.... Matter that bears spirit into the fire to be transformed: it's art. How did she know that? It was, I believe, a totally intuitive, innocent, unselfconscious, essential wisdom. And it came from a deep, innocent, unselfconscious, essential source, an essential Self. This essential

Self, I believe, belongs to each of us, and is at the same time a network, a basis of communion: my self and the Self.

When we are in touch with this stillness and this voice, we are authentic. It is our gift, and it is therefore what we have to give. We have a gift to give to one another, and we have therefore to be receptive, to be able to receive one another as gifts.

How different it would have been if I had mocked Lisa, laughed at her presumption, if I had not been able to receive what she had given me. And the poetry of it, the enlightened perception: like a Zen poet blessed with a holy vision, like a haiku: "O blessed shard, brought to the fire, to blossom a blue morning-glory."

Authenticity: what does it mean, then? That we must live and express to one another our intrinsic mysticism, our imagination. And we want to do this in order to express the world to one another in wholeness. Not only the shard, but the art of it. Not only the clay, but the spirit of it. And our imagination is a kind of sense organ that perceives the spirit as it lives in material sheaths. It perceives and it creates: imagination creates images, and it makes a difference what these images are, what they do. It makes a difference if they come from the essential Self, the networking self that carries life and truth, that carries authenticity. It's so important that we don't shortchange ourselves as less profound, less beautiful, less rare, less unique than we really are. It's self-belittling that hurts the most. How to heal it? I don't know any other way than to be continually supportive, genuine, and with respect for individual ways, both weakness and strength. Continually supportive and enthusiastic, encouraging, genuine, honestly sharing from one's own life and journey.

What are some practices to strengthen living images, in contrast to mechanical and life-destroying images? And how may thinking itself be taught in ways that promote life, rather than estrange us from it?

There's a kind of popular thinking that can be called spectator thinking: it stands apart from its object; it analyzes, documents, records. It has a kind of statistical objectivity, and as such it's been the basic discipline of higher education, turning out engineers, scientists, economists, computer specialists. And I really should say, but dread to say, teachers. This kind of thinking is not good at understanding the human soul, or at implementing creative alternatives. It tends to dry things out. Its order is mechanical rather than organic. It was developed as the appropriate coordinate of a mechanistic model of the universe: a big machine operating by mechanical laws.Results of this misconception are the pollution and destruction of the Earth, failure to have a holistic picture of the world, a failure to comprehend how toxic the invisible world has become. What we cannot see is poisoning us.

This failure is stimulating a rediscovery of life sources. And in part, this rediscovery is enabled by a thinking that participates in the formative forces of continuing creation, rather than standing apart from them.

The idea of a continuing creation was made dramatically vivid for me when I made a trip to Australia with Matthew Fox and members of his "Creation Spirituality" faculty. We flew to the outback in the center of Australia, and that encounter, and other later ones, with the aboriginal culture, led me to experience the Aboriginal Dreamtime: the dreaming. This is how they name their creation. The dreaming has brought it all about, and it is still going on. It helps to bring alive one's sense of movement right into the surfaces of rock and tree and sea and creature. Also across the land, the Aboriginals have what are called Songlines, and they sing their paths across the bush, and you'll find that when they are approaching a village, when they can barely sense its presence ahead, they will begin to sing. I said, "Why are you singing?" And they said, "Oh, it helps to bring the country up."

It helps to bring the country up. Now, music helps to make things real to us, too. We're heavily dependent on it for a sense of personal vitality and relationship. It inspires us, it helps to bring our souls into our bodies through our ears and pulse and limbs.

122

And yet, would we say so as frankly and authentically as the Australian Aboriginals? Would we say that music is part of the essential Self, that it is central to life, and therefore to education? Do we make sure that children learn the Songlines of our deeper culture? Do we practice listening and singing, not professionally, but authentically, every day?

The thinking that participates in the formative forces of continuing creation is imaginative thinking, with a strong element of empathy within it. Empathy tends toward compassion, a feeling with. Here feeling is a way of knowing, more than an emotion. We know by the feel of a thing. We may have a feeling for wholeness, before any formulation of it. Actually we may not need the formulation.

The development of a thinking that unfolds in the stages of actual living process may be fostered by a meditative observing of *Natura*. I say *Natura* instead of nature because I want to evoke a sense of the feminine and divine stature of nature. Just to follow the metamorphosis of the leaves on a buttercup, for example, takes one through a formative sequence up the stalk, which has nothing to do with logic. It has to do with the way formative energy works, how differentiation and rhythms occur, how for example leaves may become smaller as they develop further, and the surprising leap into colored petals and erect stamens. The plant goes in opposite directions simultaneously from the beginning, when the seed germinates and the root digs down into the dark earth, and the seedling leaves open up and out of it into light and air.

This principle of inherent paradox, going in opposite directions at the same moment, out of the same, as it were, cellular structure, this paradox can be understood through the geometry of the lemniscate and the Moebius strip. The lemniscate is a figure of 8, but it is a figure of 8 which is not a line but a plane, so that it has two surfaces. Therefore, if you run your finger around the top loop of the figure of 8, and your thumb is on the inside of the top loop, and you come through the crossing point and around the bottom loop, the thumb is then on the outside of the bottom loop. When you come around to the crossing point again, it's on the inside. There is this continuity of inner and outer—this brilliant geometric form, which carries this truth, which really is an integration of polarities, an integration of opposites. And it's this integration which I feel is so important for us all to learn and to teach: that the human being is also moving toward the Earth with gravity, standing on the Earth—earthlings with gravity—and also open to the heavens, with imagination, with dreams, with visions. Weightless and weighted.

I think perhaps the most important reason to keep this vividly in one's mind is that we are often asked by the culture whether we are going to be practical or visionary: just what are you going to do now, are you going to be practical or are you going to go off somewhere and be a dreamer? Well, the genius of the human being is that we are both: we're practical and we're visionary, and we mustn't be talked out of it. It's very important to keep that wholeness intact, as a picture of one's self. Or as we say, we are clay and we are word.

It may seem odd to think about clay and word both being images of creativity. But just to digress for a moment, if you look at the creation stories in our own Western scriptures, the Judeo-Christian scriptures, you find both images. In Genesis, the creation takes place with clay. The Lord breathes into the clay the spiritus, the breath/spirit. That's one version. Then in St. John's gospel, it begins, "In the beginning was the Word." What could that possibly mean? Certainly not that the Lord was using a big dictionary. But you may discover that the word that's translated as "word" is *logos*. *Logos* is a kind of mystery word. It has something to do with the principle of inner forming. With "word," you have content, you have an inner forming. And so with the clay and the word, you have that wholeness of the spirit being inwardly formed.

I live at the present time in a working community based on bio-dynamic agriculture and gardening, following suggestions made by Rudolf Steiner early in the century for the healing of the life forces of the Earth. We offer a training program for agricultural apprentices, and in it I offer a course which I call "The Renewal of Art through Agriculture." It's my purpose in this course to help the students, the farmers and gardeners, lift their perceptions into their imagination, where perceptions may be enriched by a spiritual feel and reconnected to Source. I receive some indication from these people that indeed there's a longing for this realm of experience, for this realm of universal feeling, and for the freedom to imagine what they are experiencing. All week they work with hoes and tractors, and then they come to the studio and we work with clay and color and the sounds and meanings of words.

Recently we ended a term by making clay masks, not to conceal, but to reveal the being of *Natura*, in some one of her epiphanies, happy or wounded. The masks were to be held before our faces and spoken through. What would these beings say? They were nodes on the life line of the great tree of life: they spoke of connection and disconnection, of ecstatic union and grief-stricken destruction. The masks were the countenances of *Natura*'s living aspects.

Being thus ensourced, art is renewed, and along with the art, the artist's person: we were renewed, deepened, made more reflective, made more acute in our listening to one another, more astounded in our beholding, simpler in our stories, as we heard their divine genesis.

At the end of the session, the students lingered, they didn't want to leave: they didn't want to leave that world of the imagination which they'd helped to create, and which felt so alive and juicy and touching. They know they can't live without it.

The Earth is dying because we have not been able to cross over into the double realm: we've been doing the tasks of materialism cut off from spirit. Now the bonds are loosening, an evolutionary step is being taken, we are reentering, rediscovering, renewing, recreating. We may be open to a transformation of our thinking, of our way of conceiving the world: imagination is opening us with pictures and images; inspiration is responding to our revitalized listening; intuition receives us into a union and interdependence, a wholeness.

The child in us tends to know these things already. Perhaps that's why she tends to be so abused in our culture. The child is witness to another realm that challenges our will to control and to dominate. Often in ourselves there is this severe conflict between our mystical child and the educated adult we have become, between the mystical and the secular souls in our own breasts. Part of what one hopes to do with one's poetry and one's life is to awaken imagination as the light that can shine within all one's behavior and experience, to bring the mystical awe into the secular cynicism and despair, to lift the hoe and the tractor into wands and divine engines, to live in the real world.

Remember the cautionary story of the Zen sage who said, "Now that I'm enlightened I'm just as miserable as ever." Suffering is not eliminated by imagination. It is beheld in its colors and in its meaning. Another practice which may strengthen the forms of personal knowing, personal gnosis, is creativity. Creativity opens us to the offerings of the creative unconscious. From artistic mind, from the realm of growth and becoming, out of which forms arise. These offerings from spirit source are intrinsic to ourselves; they are not difficult to come by. They may be asleep and need to be awakened, or wounded and need to be healed, or repressed and need to be slowly and gently invited and exercised.

T.S. Eliot said that humankind cannot bear very much reality. What he may have meant is that it can be surprisingly painful and even disorienting to look in the mirror and see one's original face, so different from the one we prepare, as Eliot says, to meet the faces that we meet. Practicing creativity may develop courage and honesty and compassion, tenderness for those sensitive expressions of our inner selves, our hopes and fears and dreams, our observations and experiences—this is a realm and an activity for receptivity, not for aesthetic judgment, good, bad, best and so on.

In my workshops, I try not to allow participants to compare their work with someone else's, or to make jokes about how it looks. These habits of defensive chatter have to be overcome. One has gradually to grow comfortable in the stillness that surrounds the piece. Remember Lisa, and the dignity of that little pot shard. "It's art," she said solemnly.

My intention is to protect the creative experience from random violence. For it is our authenticity that is beginning to be revealed and to function creatively. It is a precious smoldering core, the basis for a passionate community of creative individuals in whom the archetypal world is reflected. When we have access to this world, through our unconscious senses—unconscious to ordinary mind, conscious to intuitive mind—we may decide which divinity we mean to serve. The Self that connects within and without is our authenticity. When we play with the primary material, like clay or fiber or color or movement or sound or speech—we are activating our connection with the archetypal world, the great sources of universal imagery. We can come to greater self-knowledge, seeing what we make, feeling our souls moving through our hands. We can come to know ourself as a human person, a shared nature and a shared community and a unique being. These become our authenticity, out of which we may live and work and create and suffer and enrich the soil for others by our becoming part of it.

Thomas Berry calls himself a geologian—combining perhaps the geo of Earth and theologian. He is part of the deep ecology impulse and a participant in the Creation Spirituality program. In *The Dream of the Earth*, Berry speaks of authenticity:

The ecological age fosters the deep awareness of the sacred presence within each reality of the universe. There is an awe and reverence due to the stars in the heavens, the Sun, and all heavenly bodies; to the seas and the continents; to all living forms of trees and flowers, to the myriad Expressions of life in the sea; to the animals of the forests and the birds of the air. To wantonly destroy a living species is to silence forever a divine voice. Our primary need for the various life-forms of the planet is a psychic, rather than a physical, need. The ecological age seeks to establish and maintain this subjective identity, this authenticity at the heart of every being....

This identity carries with it an interior depth of special quality, a mystery that expresses not only a phenomenal mode but also an archetypal realization. This enables each articulation of the real to resonate with that numinous mystery that pervades all the world. This quality of things is universal but its activation in the human order provides the creative dynamics of the thinker, the poet, the writer, the scientist, the farmer, the educator and whichever other role is fulfilled by human beings in the functioning of the universe.

To repeat that key sentence:

THE ECOLOGICAL AGE SEEKS TO ESTABLISH AND MAINTAIN THIS SUBJECTIVE IDENTITY, THIS AUTHENTICITY AT THE HEART OF EVERY BEING.

Now I will read two or three poems which I hope will bear upon our theme:

LOVE POEMS

"I believe the appropriate symbol of the Cosmic Christ who became incarnate in Jesus is that of Jesus as Mother Earth crucified yet rising daily." (Matthew Fox)

"Jesus is our true Mother in whom we are endlessly carried and out of whom we will never come." (Julian of Norwich)

Deep Ecology

Christ's blood is green
in the branches,
blue in the violet.
Her bright voice
laughs in the night wind.
The big nova swells
in her breast.
Christ suckles us
with spring sap and
spreads earth under our feet.

O she loves us,
feeds us, tricks us with
her triple ways:
calls us soul,
calls us body, and spirit.
Calls us to her bed.

Liturgy

O I touch and am touched
by the smouldering core of you.
The colors that surface in your flesh
carry my sight into the temple beyond seeing.
My heart is pounding, impatient for the sacrament
that changes our bodies into communion.
You are my door. Through you
I am entered.

This poem expresses the authenticity of the sacred beyond gender! The essential Self carries in it the vision of all genders: to know oneself or another at a depth before body and to feel how that being of oneself takes on body male and female. And there is the essential play of left and right, of conscious and unconscious; the unconscious of the woman is male, the unconscious of the male is female. We can begin to dissolve the ignorant assumptions about identity and embodiment. We meet one another and the world at the Source.

It's challenging to live at this level; we aren't used to it and bring to it attitudes and habits no longer appropriate. There's one striking feature of this realm of authenticity. Rudolf Steiner clarified it for me by observing that in the spiritual world, the world of authenticity, of true values and of compassion, everything is just the opposite of what we have come to on the materialistic plane. For example, for one's essential Self, the values of pride, vanity, greed, anxiety are not present. To the inner eye of personal direct knowing, free of cultural programming, values are imaginative, creative, just, equitable, humorous. One rejoices in one's luck at being alive, awestruck by the beauty and the pain, patient with impatience.

Why is authenticity so difficult in popular culture? There are powerful forces working against it: social pressure, habits, shallow commitment. Sophistication.

This is a new time. The Earth is ready to make love with us. Let's offer her our joy in our true selves.

POET

I put on my poet's shirt
and birds fly through.
Birds perch in me and
their throats tremble.
Their high singing builds
in me a listening love.

Clothes are the sheaths
of my being — so many old dreams of
changing dress, unable to decide,
always late for the occasion,
what to wear?

Now the dreamer is at rest:
she wears the nests, the eaves
and orchards. Wears the tall pine
of the white-throated sparrow
in the city walk-up — the gutters
and sills — understanding a language
she does not know, hearing the inaudible.

POTTER

This flat plate. This ladle and bowl.
Clay whirled on a wheel, raised slowly to the table.
Straight and curved, our primal gestures
take and give — speak out about
the way we stand and breathe.
Every leaf is saucer for the bread.
Every falling drop prepares its cup.
Always we are eating and drinking earth's body,
Making her dishes.
Potters like sun and stars
perform their art —
endowed with myth,
they make the meal holy.

PELTED BY BEAUTY
(after an American Indian Flower Ritual)

The power of love received in the body: This was the Festival!
      how we stood and faced one another
          and we took hands,
          and the love came.
And all the flowers swarmed about our heads:
          deep deep the sting goes.
Let love be welcomed the moment it seeks us.

In my flesh I feel it still,
      the surprise and awe, the joy,
    warming and swelling in my limbs and belly,
      O miraculous conception O angels tumbling through the air!
How real it is, the Christscript branded across our lips:
        that we shall love one another—as if the world could ever be the same.
      Over the edge, into the well, the abyss,
          idiotically amorous,
      nibbling at the green fronds and flinging them!
Pelted by beauty and peace,
      a cellular reordering, each tiny vessel
      lovecrazed, opening.
The fountain erupts, cascades,
and we wish to die in it, be other,
be one in an alchemy of eros,
that lad with the arrows who shoots blind.

The power of love is received in the body,
      our first and primal home.
Not enough is made of incarnation, the mysteries of birth,
      of embodiments here like this *in* one another:
        your eyes and my arched back,
          our fingers softening.

Of course now we dance differently,
    bowing and dipping and turning to the delicate drum.
Of course we live now in the dread of our disguises.
      We know our body and offer it,
    We know our need and carry our begging bowl.

Now hear with courage our own love cries,
the tender shout of readiness, yes,
I will, I do, yes, let us receive into our bodies
    the divine pulse, anointed with petals,
awaken and go forth changed.

        Now truly are we god's fools,
lilies of the field, no thought for the morrow,
feeding strangers and comforting the fearful,
doing good to those who hurt us,
carrying blossoms to beat beauty and peace into our bones.

    This poem was written after an American Indian flower ritual was performed. At its climax, a huge basket of flowers was poured over the poet's head, engulfing her in their multifloriate rapture. It was she who was being celebrated in this ritual, and it was she therefore who had to be most deeply pelted, nay, pulverized by beauty! It was a magical ecstasy, moving, as the poem sings, through the body into a new behavior.

The Renewal of Art
through Agriculture

I have painted the female hills
stretched and piled against the sky.
They are sleeping.
I have given them golden haloes.
They are saints.
They are sleeping.
I have painted the gold in clouds and crevices as well,
meaning to say how they too are saints,
how the world sleeps,
how womanly is the landscape,
how a whiskered angel also sleeps
as a field of grain.

I give a course in Pennsylvania in the Kimberton Hills agricultural program which I call "The Renewal of Art through Agriculture." It is an intuitive thrust toward re-imaging the farmer and the processes of art. I am an artist, and I use the materials of clay, color, words in the creativity workshop which I offer. I am passionate about agriculture as a priority in this time of social and political and ecological commitment: biodynamic agriculture. Rudolf Steiner, Austrian scientist and seer (1861–1925), gave the original agriculture course to farmers in Koberwitz in 1924. The picture of the farmer, the farm, the Earth, the cosmos which he depicts is a part of a total perception of Nature and human destiny. The whole is felt in every part. Steiner called this new wisdom, or renewed wisdom, Anthroposophy: Its purpose is to reconnect spirit in the human being with spirit in the universe.

To heal the division. To experience life-spirit in the sense-perceptible world. It is what Steiner called a new clairvoyance suitable for our time. For it applies the disciplines of natural science to the new picture.

The experience of art is an experience of transcendence through the senses. That is why the artist in each person is to be nourished and valued. It is a way of experiencing connection and meaning.

Art is spiritual perception. It delivers the perception to us through color in painting or glass, through still life, portraiture, landscape, through the energy of color fields touching. Through music, through sound. Through dance, through drama, through sculpture and drawing and architecture. Through craftart. The artist within us expresses our intuitive fire—part of the original fireball—moments when we feel the burning contact. We don't have to justify it or explain it. We have only to give it, and the giving is itself a kind of receiving from Source. It is a communion uniting inner and outer.

Art is spiritual perception, and its organ is imagination. How do we school imagination, awaken it, encourage it, support its activities and insights? Agriculture is a schooling for spiritual perception. For it is there that we learn to practice meditative attention: the detailed observation of the living process. We begin to be able to see "signs of life" before they are fully visible, and signs of decay in the rhythms of work. Artistic "work" combines observation and intuitive improvisation as a way of integrating life-presence and wisdom, allowing it to surface. We gain in confidence and boldness and authenticity. Our sense of self and the truth of things unite.

I will give a few examples of the kinds of experiences I invite the students into. When the crocuses come up, we may go outside with paper and colored pencils, to "draw" them—that is, to make with color on the page in a way that evokes "crocus" to each of us. We know that we are not being asked simply to draw the shape of the flower, but to feel the movement of the pencil connected with the formative activity of the plant. Its edge is the border of its becoming. The entity of the flower is immanent in its growth and blooming and fading, like an invisible substance manifesting in line and color. We may call this substance the etheric body of the crocus. It moves fluidly through the forms of the plant, extending beyond its physical borders, softening them. We are learning to perceive these fields of etheric formative forces.

And then we write some of the feelings we have had in the presence of this being.

> Delicate sticky fragile
> flowers
> Spikey spidery delicate leaves
> A cold spell will wilt them
> They welcome warmth.
> . . .
> The bees were mostly inside
> the crocuses that were
> only one color. But the
> crocuses that were only one
> color had shadows of
> great variety.
> . . .
> Delicately perfectly purple,
> attracting me as well as the bees!

We learn to see and to feel at the same time. We learn to be participants, not spectators.

Another time we may work with clay to express time through space. We can hint at geological changes in the Earth's surface. We can suggest the development of character in a face, or decrepitude in a body. The images that come are various, surprising. I ask the students to paint the clay with the acrylic paint I use. Immediately the images become more magical, more vividly seen and deeply felt. Landscape is so much a part of the farmer's art. And color is a doorway to the mysteries of feeling.

Time may also be experienced through color and color changes. Again with colored pencils we evoke the course of the day, from dawn to twilight, in a wide horizontal band, beginning at one end with dawn and following the colors of the day in whatever season it is. It is important for the farmer/artist to watch the sky and to read its face: the clouds, the light and shadows, the stars. We would like to develop the kind of nose for weather that an animal has, not only daily weather but developing weather. What will the winter be like? The spring? When light first appears at dawn, what color is it? Why? How do we read color in fruit? I once arranged a still life of apples and asked the class to give it creative expression in any way they chose. I myself made a clay sculpture of the group and painted it. I still have it. The apples seem sublime, eternal, cast in rock, some kind of miracle one can bite into and taste on another plane.

In the fall, after the sowing of the rye, we come into the studio and repeat the movements of our bodies and arms as we walked the field and spread the grain. We feel the gestures of this ritual, the arc and trajectory of the seeds as they fall from our hands, the total picture of movement and meaning. This is theater, this is dance and drama. And we may take large sheets of paper and make "drawings" of this soaring and whirling and grounded experience. It is a way of internalizing this ritual practice and of sharing our awe.

Art in our culture is often despairing, unsure, or aggressive. It is often sharp-tongued, greedy, brash, self-conscious, impotent, ambitious, desperate for attention, yet insecure, for reward, for a sense of self, for meaning—heartbroken, withdrawn. This is what I find in students, who tend to come both hopeful and hopeless. Professional art has become part of the money economy. We hear less about beauty and more about prices. I am as committed to the essential value and priority of creativity as to agriculture. We must find our way to our original face, our original Source, and no longer be tempted to betray it. We need to practice "making new," making original, making true, making connections, making deep ecology and deep ecumenism.

Spiritual presence can be experienced as one finds one's own voice in harmony with cosmic wisdom, which is the book of Nature, of stars, the seasons. It is the book of agriculture, the "culture" of soil life. What else is there to study but the ground under our feet—as it drinks and dries, receives and offers, engenders and engulfs? What else is there but agriculture to feed us, and if we are not fed, what then?

Art is a feeding. The contemporary world is starved and starving. We suffer from soul malnutrition (which is probably connected to the toxic food we get from widespread chemical farming). This is why we cannot easily laugh nor love nor leap nor rest.

The Renewal of Art through Agriculture! Let the apprentices learn a different way of looking—to see the images of art coming from the depths of dawn and dusk, the rituals of animal care, of sowing and reaping, of digging and harvesting—an imaginative shout of gold across the field as the hay ripens to its cutting. How the gold gilds farmer and wagon and air! To see color as presence, Nature as presence, to hear sounds as meaning. ("Everything in the world has a spirit that is released by its sound." This remark excited composer John Cage's imagination: it set him on fire.) To gather the carbon and silica, calcium, nitrogen, oxygen and hydrogen and iron in a vivid communion of our chemical brothers and sisters.

"The living world" awaits us, "living process." The Australian Aboriginal "Dreamtime," a time of continuous creation, awaits us. All our relations (as Native Americans pray) await us.

When I returned from Australia in 1990 I told my class that I felt now I understand what our course is about; I learned it from the Aboriginals, from their participation in Nature and spirit. Levi Strauss, the anthropologist, called it "participation mystique," the intuitive union of person and planet.

These resources of intuition and inspiration, along with imagination, can be called forth and empowered. We need places to practice the new ecological consciousness, the new clairvoyance (seeing into the processes of becoming), the new meditative alliance with concentration: think soft, unthink, receive, be supple in your listening, and *respond.*

The world needs our response out of our listening and receiving and observing. Our direct perception and our participation. The world needs farmers as stewards of life process, of our daily bread. The grain and the grape: a cosmic communion, a daily sacrament. We behold our work as upon an altar.

We give our work as we give our love, our attention. We need to ask for gifts in return. It is the fundamental social law: to give and to receive. We do not work for wages, we work to provide what our brothers and sisters need. They cannot buy our diligence and devotion. They give us gifts. Farming cannot be economically "sound," nor can art. They are gifts, and they will be supported by gifts from those who receive them. It is a new human consciousness and social order.

Biodynamic farming and gardening is never just technical. Its purpose is also to create vision in a community through educational and vocational work. The biodynamic farm organism works not only in the soil but in the soul. It impacts on the economic, social, psychological life of a community. And the education of the farmer has as its ultimate goal not only the healing of the soil and the growing of food, but the development of rural culture. The Rural Development Service Group located in Las Vegas, New Mexico, is courageously beginning a program which will help both the Spanish-speaking and English-speaking populations to find their way to a renewed agricultural resource and cultural vision.

The Renewal of Art through Agriculture is a call not only to the creative self but to the socially conscious self and its energized relationship to others. There is a new view to be birthed, and a new practice. A view of the world as person, of Nature as presence, of agriculture as ritual and prayer, and of farmers as initiates who will renew art as a life-inspired vocation.

Creativity and
the Practice of Awe

To behold with awe is to see things filled with their own light, their own Bit of Being, and to be moved by a sense of the numinous. This light and this bit of being are gifts of creation. As gifts they fill us with awe. This awe is accompanied by delight. It is the original blessing.

To feel the divine in all things is a real challenge, especially when an experience is painful and confusing—or when we are asked to accept with joy something we have never felt close to. Certain specific personal experiences have brought me recently to a perception of AWE that can be the ground of social justice and of grief work. AWE is more than a perception, it is a feeling. It is personal. It starts with our own breath. It makes mystics of us.

I want to begin by describing the experiences which set in motion this wish to speak with you about the practice of AWE. Since AWE is a basic element of the four paths of Creation Spirituality, how do we learn to practice it in our lives? If we don't feel it, how can it be awakened? Art as meditation is meant to be a birthing of AWE, and Creativity brings us again and again to the edge of wonder and worship, to the edge of mystery. Immersion in wonder and mystery may become ways of behaving in the world, may become practice and commitment, which may help to bring about transformation in our lives and in society.

The first experience occurred very unexpectedly. It was a bit of a shock. It really attracted my attention! A group of students and friends had gathered to discuss the question of WORK—of vocation. What is work? How does one find Good Work? How does one find a work that satisfies?

I asked if I might say something about my lifestyle—about the choices I have made about work. I live in a community with disabled adults, based on biodynamic agriculture and social therapy. Our work consists of gardening and farming: greenhouse, vegetables, herbs, field crops, cows, sheep, orchard, vineyard, and so on.; 460 acres, about 120 souls, including children of co-workers. Our labor is also in the houses: preparing meals, preserving and freezing fresh food crops, caring for the house and the human relationships. This is the social therapy: healing through creating community. This is the goal. There is also artistic work, and free play.

I spoke enthusiastically about the garden, about weeding the strawberries and picking the string beans. The response to this was, "But isn't that rather menial?" I was dumbfounded. Menial? I had to look the word up in the dictionary, suddenly unsure of what it actually means. What it means is "low on the employment scale." Socially inferior work—without status. Farm work. Seasonal work. Physical work serving basic needs. MENIAL!

I was utterly unprepared for the chasm that opened between my assumptions and those of my students and friends. How could it be that they were not ecstatic as I am about the wonders of a garden, the amazing generosity of nature in providing food in all colors and shapes and sizes—just for the planting, cultivating, and harvesting—the WORK! Isn't food itself AWE-INSPIRING?

The question haunted me. It seemed to be a riddle which, if solved, might contain a clue about social prejudice. If the divine is to be found in all things, what are the forces that conspire to exclude certain kinds of work and certain kinds of workers?

There is a need to broaden our sense of what constitutes social justice. How can social justice be implemented by a more embracing attitude?

The answer came. What was missing was AWE! My friends felt no AWE as they beheld a strawberry forming, or held the long slender envelope of a bean. Nor do they feel AWE before the field workers and home gardeners who provide cities and neighborhoods with fresh food. This is meant to be a statement of fact, not a criticism or a scolding. The fact is, weeding strawberries and picking beans does not turn them on, either to do it or to see it being done. Farming is not a work that would qualify on their list of options.

How do we increase the scope of our AWE?

The second encounter which has triggered this "recovery of AWE" is with death. I have suffered more deaths of loved ones this year than I can handle. One is too much. A beloved is suddenly gone without a trace. Where is she? How has that dear form been translated into "dust"? I don't get it. I don't like it. Death is too much for me. Not my own, that doesn't seem to be a problem. But my friends. All that sweetness gone.

The answer to this riddle is, I submit, AWE. I had lost my AWE before death. I kept asking it to make sense, to shape up, to explain itself, to justify itself. It was out of my control. And suddenly I fell off the edge into Mystery. MYSTERY! Death is a mystery. It is too big, too unfathomable, for any of us to grasp. To allow it to become a deposit in the soul is intolerable. It must be dissolved, dissolved again and again, by silent AWE as the great archetype moves relentlessly among us. Mystery, a meditation, a shroud, a sound that is both Lamentation and Praise.

AWE is the ground of social justice and grief work. That's my offering.

How can AWE become a spiritual practice, a discipline? How can it become a commitment, a spiritual work, a behavior? If we don't already feel it, how can we awaken it?

A friend who is in a twelve-step program gave me the following tip: if there is a step you should be taking (like making a relationship to God) and you aren't there yet, you "fake it till you make it." You behave "as if." Oh, wonderful! It's one way to change a habit. We can inhibit the old hang-up, and practice the new. The Irish poet Yeats talks about wearing the golden mask. I take this to mean something similar. Wear the mask of perfection and grow into it.

Some might say this is hypocritical—but that is not the spirit behind it. The spirit is more like Robert Browning's line "Our reach should exceed our grasp/ or what's a heaven for?" Of course, as soon as we are in sync with the new work, we are in a new place in ourselves.

Creativity in the arts can be the practice field for AWE. Working with a primary material, like clay, wood, stone, metals, fiber, glass, movement, sound, speech, brings us again and again to the edge of wonder and discovery. How can it be that there should now be this image where before there was nothing? I make a mark on the ground or on a page. A hermit crab drops tiny pellets. Lightning makes a long black scar down a tree trunk. All the things that I can do and make are values: round, square, pointed, rough, smooth, torn, pinched, squeezed, smoothed, broken and mended. Beholding them as births, as gifts, as surprises, brings us to AWE.

Creativity is like the original flaring-forth. It is not judgmental, is not aesthetic, is not critical. Moral objections to creative acts tend to come from transgression of cultural taboos, or illness, or physical abuse. There are no absolutes here.

Think of creativity as gift—a gift to oneself, gift to others. Not as achievement, not competitive. Innocent, like the widow's mite. Like the child who comes running with its latest scribble or mud-pie and says SEE WHAT I MADE, IT'S FOR YOU! Awe, delight, love! Rub color on paper and feel awe at the birthing of beauty as the color is revealed.

Thinking that one is not artistic means not including oneself in the practice of AWE. We open our arms, we stretch the clay little by little. We make our mark on the body of the Earth. It is praise and celebration. It is not always cheerful, it is sometimes a confession of pain. Pain is divine too—it is a sign of consciousness. Certainly the gods feel it. We feel our pain on behalf of mindfulness, on behalf of healing, on behalf of sacrifice, of making sacred.

Transformation is the final path in Creation Spirituality. To transform vision into behavior is an ideal we serve. The human being is made up of opposites, is at home in opposites. We are both visionaries and activists. We have our feet on the ground and our head full of imagination. We live both outside and inside when we are whole. Integration is an archetypal labor of our time. Consciousness work is such a labor, and body work is such a labor. Integrating consciousness and the body is one of our opportunities. Opening, softening, focusing, letting go: these can be our practices.

AWE is the basic connection between humans and the cosmos. It is the standard by which we measure our receptivity ... to Work, to Grief, to Love, to Creativity.

—1994

PERSON OF COLOR. 1994. Acrylic on paper. 32″ x 40″

WINGED SEED. 1989. Acrylic on paper. 5′ x 5′

RELEASE AND TRANSFORMATION. 1991. Acrylic on paper. 34″ x 48″
One of three paintings on the beheading of John the Baptist.

POET. 1994. Acrylic on paper. 36″ x 45″

BEFORE THE BEGINNING

New Poems by M.C. Richards

1991 – 1996

Valentine Haiku for Matthew Fox
(after Meister Eckhart)

Baby, you iz.
As God iz, so iz you.
As you iz, so God's iz iz.

Sweet Corn

Yesterday I was shucking corn
for supper — pulling off the green sheaths
and brushing away the silks —
and suddenly in my hand I feel the naked cob
so cool, sweet, intimate, smooth, like skin I'm holding.
And I am deeply touched with surprise and rapture.

And I think how it is to feel life in the skin,
in the touch of plant flesh (sweet milk swelling the seeds) —
and how mostly people go for days
without touching anything from the earth
that lives in its skin, but mostly they are touching
metal, glass, plastic, formica, concrete, newspaper,
not a moment of rapture
as in the everyday glisten of sweet corn.

That it should be an EAR I'm holding!
How to fathom the image, how to fill the resonant spaces,
the cantata of its inwardness. Like ivory keys
I play the kernels with my tongue:
    OH
    OH

August 24, 1994
Kimberton Hills, Pennsylvania

Eco-lalia

I am sitting in a lawn chair
 in late afternoon August sun
and suddenly I am covered with butterflies
 kissing me with their tiny mouths
and their needle tools probing my pores for nectar.
  Their wings are a subtle murmur, moving the air like fur.
  Out of my fingers bloom Roses of Sharon,
and in the bush shines a face of deep amethyst.

 Oh shining cattle
 Oh grass matted and fish wet in our thighs
and pine branches tangled at Venus Mount,
 the rocky ridges of our spines,
the caves of marrow.
 Clay between our toes
and from our ears an untrimmed wick.
 Oh feel your antlered skull,
 your rage of ocean depths,
 the harvest of night.

This grasshopper, green and heedless, blesses its destiny.
The geese of imagination fly north to nest and drowse.
Our skin is white water, fresh and porous.
The mammoth is our circus, the ibis our requiem.

We are a new species:
whose hands bloom
whose spirit hovers like a water bird
whose tongue flashes fire
and who feeds like lichen on stones.

August 25, 1994
Kimberton Hills, Pennsylvania

148

Why Do We Think
We Have Not Been Here All Along?

Who has made the polar bear?
I, said Jane, I made the bear,
she slept in my pocket.
And who made the hare? I,
said the sculptor, who else would dare?

Before the beginning we slept
in each other's arms and dreamed
the universe.
All together we have created this evolving world.

In deep spirit recesses,
we birth the laws: blood warmth,
and beat, imagination, breath,
awe as separateness and connection fuse.

The textures of this world imagine themselves:
    still births and love affairs,
    glaciers, lava, elephant and fly.
The sweep of orange through the evening sky
    from its own brush.
Hawk and fieldmouse are mirrored
    in each other's eye.

So intimate is our kinship to parsnip and clover,
to hunger and harvest, so pure is my recognition
of YOU yes this am I,
why do we think we have not been here all along?

August 29, 1994
Kimberton, Pennsylvania

149

Notes from an Aboriginal Walkabout
in West Australia

(I am chock full of unspent passion
and undigested perceptions.
I need to lay some stuff out:)

Frans with the goldgrey desert in his hair,
the lean laugh of the adopted aboriginal,
curtained in green silk from the sun —
in the sand his finger draws the law,
draws the manifestation — click click
the little boomerangs in the singing.

The broad white plain of sand, the gnarled red rock
and grit, the dust — how our bodies drink
the moonlight, burn in its white ochre flame,
how we ready ourselves for sleep as if
lying in the palm of a soft hand — letting go
of the emptiness, feeling the still heart rest
and fill with new senses. Spit in the hard clay
to soften it, spit in the ground stone ochre for paint,
become the water we seek, become the wallaby,
the banksia, the ember saved for the next fire.

The song line, the song line, singing the country up:
the song of the grassy hump, the water hole, the big stone,
I want to hear the songs, I want to be the songs,
I am drawn to the spirit of their singing as by a magnet,
I am drawn like the thread from a spider's belly
connecting in a great web tender and tough and transitory
and permanent as granite in the soul's eye. I lust
for this green emerald of the sea that shines in their
dark eyes — lust for the phallus of their memory,
the vulva of their hearing — O yes the great mother organ,

the great pouch, into which they receive what has been created,
their joey,[1] their perfected instinct. I lust
and cannot be quieted easily — until I have sat in the dirt
enough to be changed into dust, and to feel on my eyes
the spittle of spirit, to open and be new.

To have nothing but what you intrinsically are,
ah! No cup, no spoon, no trousers, no house, no car,
no insurance, no books, no canned goods, no money —
nothing owned, nothing that is mine and not also yours.

Perhaps possession and attachment and greed and
envy and competition and tyranny have to be learned —
perhaps love can be learned as well,
    for love is a winged changeling and cannot be captured
in a phrase: must fly, and crouch / and cover, and uncover/
must offer, and remain silent / must touch, and live
transparent to touching / must trod heavily shod, and
yet be homeless as the wind. To be homeless and free
to become one another /

                          free to be the wind blowing where
it listeth, free to receive the law.

Coastal tribes walked these beaches of West Australia
feeding on bush tucker[2] and communications of divine Oneness.
Feeding and being fed. Hearing in their inner ear
the stories of destiny, retelling them, learning the living
languages of earth's creatures, perfecting their ear for
meaning. Can you hear me, O aboriginal sister and brother?
Do you hear our cry for help, our readiness to give what we
have and follow you? Where shall we come, through the eye
of the needle? Around what corner will our hope bring us
to your dark radiance?

---

1. Baby kangaroo.
2. Wild food.

You live in the spiritual world, and it is there we
are called to enter. We are called to live in community
with fellow beings — ready to translate the values of worldly
culture into life and truth. So much to unlearn. So much
to practice anew. So much to love.

Around the edge of the coast the earth's aura shows
through the layers of bluegreen water: an aura of
tawny golden brown and red ochre and yellow in subtle colors,
a subtle breathing out into the deep and into the core.
When I lie on the ground in the bush I feel this breathing.
Here now through the cement floor in my American room
I feel its insistence.

Ab originale, that is, *from the beginning, from source.*
Let us receive the gift of our aboriginality and welcome it
into our behavior. Amen.

Oct 17, 1993

Shining Hands

This hand flickers at my lips,
this hand falls to its knees and bows,
two hands drum time out of silence.
Like flowers they open and close.
Soul flows down my arm, blood-warmth
in my fingers.
O hand at my breast, you teach love.
You guide our spoons into our mouths.
You free an angel from marbled rock.
O heart, out of your deep dark
our hands carry light into this world.

April 27, 1995

The Movies

His hands all over her,
back and front, side to side,
squeezing her buttocks, mounting,
coming into her, tender, passionate,
heavy male body; under her skirts
on the floor as she plays the piano;
caressing the back of her neck,
his fingers under her blouse...
What am I to do with all this,
all these images? What am I to do
with the strong dream of you
kissing me so long it wakes me
to this empty room. Your dream lips
are full and soft. In life
you peck drily.

What am I to do with these invasions
of love and pain — my skin so hungry —
haunted by the naked lover dusting the piano,
rubbing it slowly deeply.
I am here at the window watching a hummingbird
probing for nectar in the bark of an old fir tree.

What am I to do with the grief of death?

January 14, 1994

153

Morning Notes

This is such a nice typewriter
I wish I had something to say.
Let's see: a college campus
dorm room
                   many young voices
hollering "happy birthday" in the night,
like Basho's frog in the pond
suddenly BELLY FLOP.

A big evergreen tree outside my window,
its roots mumble under the surface.
A long concrete divider,
steps 3 at a time,
sky cloudy and heavy
squeezing a thin layer of light against the city,
the first red leaves of an otherwise green shrub.

The sisters are gone from the convent, the dancers
     are gone from the hill,
morning has come to its noon.
The hide of the tree has grown rough scales,
the trunk bends its hip to the left and
shakes its disheveled branches
to a secret music of release.

Morphology

The usual mess on the desk top —
Turn my head and it's dapple everywhere:
   under the tree, across the pavement.

Under the mess, the dapple sleeps,
and dreams — a muted radiance
but there.
Morphology: how things are made,
how they come about, how they are named.
When we don't know, we cry CHAOS!
It is a prayerful outcry, naming
the unnameable, seeing how we are made:
how we are connected: how through the mess
a torrent of angelic silence spills,
how we are wet with its shine — how
our morphology dances its dapple.

Strawberry

In November
the strawberry hangs on a thread of sleep.
In May
it lies in my hand like an erotic dream.

In the Garden

In the garden the wild mind buds and swells
with words that cannot rest, cannot be spelled,
that turn this pink, this lemon yellow,
the color speechless saying,
"Here here the language lives intense,
love lifts its hues like sentences that sculpt the soul."
Oh how to say it,
how to bend with the words' weight yet feel them fly
in brushstrokes purple and mint and magenta and blue
completing a phrase.
    Veils of color pulse in the mind,
become syllables and tones, a music that dissolves,
makes us stutter into trills and birdsongs,
turns us loose, wilderness at play.
The player is our soul in its garden,
where words bud in the bright mouths of spring.

Red Is a Presence

Red is a presence. Here
it is holding a green moon.
It is not a surface, it is a
being.
        Apricot gold washes the petals,
gilds their mysterious service
gathering like an egg the fertile glory.
The sharp green strikes
long and hard the vertical
stretch of branch and twig —
the blue recedes, leaves its mantle behind,
lowers its eyes, comes away oh away.
The black brush sweeps its ink
in a wild mood of the cipher:
color, you are!
    You call us into movement and stillness,
you carve vessels and
speak in tongues. Your arms reach
into hell, and into heaven.
    I cannot find the picture
without your innuendo, your changing
changelessness.
    Banish the image and release the soul
ready to spring into hue and tint. Dissolve,
dissolve, make the way free to the next
changeling. Be the hen
walking the tightrope fence.
Disappear! Be the stirring grass,
be the single white clover, be the motionless
sky changing invisibly invisibly. Grey
engulfs the immense horizon, nothing
happens, everything is happening. We are
a theater of time and color.

How slowly it overtakes us,
this theater piece. How slowly the night
comes and goes, the dark paints itself
indigo and silver; blue and yellow the stars,
they do not fade but slowly erase themselves,
make aquamarine, make violet,
make green, muddying the blue
into brown and purple. Where is the edge,
when will it come to its edge and turn back?
When will it be limb and leaf and countenance?
When dissolve into the original palette?
    We do not make "exercises" out of
the presence of God.
We praise, we adore, we are fearful,
we are upheld.
Look, everywhere the sheaths are shattered,
the color is essence. It carries the mark
of matter, known by its own voice.
How sweet is the colorless void,
the gathering of poppies, the both/and
truth that transcends form. Yet the form
lives in the arm that paints, the soul that
sees the angels densely struggling
as human passion engraves its love
and frees it into color.

Dream #1

The blue sky lies billowing on the land
and we are walking in it, blue sand.
Overhead crimson and ivory of pomegranates.
As we walk, bright crystals shine like stars
in the blue ground under our feet.
A crazed moon crackles in a juniper bush.
We see a few tents, a small village, and go that way.
It is the new earth.

Suddenly, I take your arm.

They Are Sleeping

I have painted the female hills
stretched and piled against the sky.
They are sleeping.
I have given them golden haloes.
They are saints.
They are sleeping.
I have painted the gold in clouds and crevices as well,
meaning to say how they too are saints,
how the world sleeps,
how womanly is the landscape,
how a whiskered angel also sleeps, as a field of grain.

For Burt the Temple Dancer

You were dancing in the temple
when you fell
between the money changers and the mills of the gods
grinding down the tracks.
You had just planted a tree on the altar
and a line of evergreens down the nave.
The knees of your costume were brown and wet
with the soil you had been kneeling in.
On your knees, on your knees, digging
the womb for the new root, the bulb,
crazy with deep semen laughter, in a continuing
fertility gavotte.
I lost you for a moment, you vanished so fast,
I was dizzy and nauseous in the spinning
walkway, the acceleration of time, it was too soon too soon
for you to die. Die was not a word that fit you
in any way.
    Now I know where you are:
you are where the colors are
before they come onto my canvas —
you are where the sounds rise in a realm
before the throat — the words
before we speak them — the lengthening of your arm
before it moves into its new stretch.
You are there where we are when we are artists and
the Muse has taken us, when we can feel
there is something from the other side coming through.
    I found you suddenly, suddenly you and I
were in the same timeless spaceless dance. I
was painting. I had turned to the colors
in my grief. I moved the brush.
Yellow, magenta, olive, sienna, gold, rose.
I felt myself change.

The ecstasy spread up my wrists.
The edges of my body softened.
There you appeared, intent and buoyant.
We entered the sanctum together
and knew where we were, where we are.

—1992

A Love Poem for Dartmoor
(during an outing, April 21, 1993)

This wild dark desert, bright with day —
black dirt like rough silk between my fingers,
purple lichen and marsh violets —
golden bowels of wandering cows, those vagrant pilgrims
begging their alms of grass, clear streams, and azure sky,
grey and moist with shadow.
   We walk here uplifted by the spongy turf,
challenged by the granite Tor and the stretch of emptiness.
We rest in the folds of your garment.
   Our signal is a rock phallus standing in a birthing pool with stone fish,
a Celtic wedding of Eros and Sophia.
   A stone circle stands rooted like teeth in a
great jaw carved to speak the unutterable
primal ceremonies.
   And the yellow-tipped gorse
makes jaunty lamps in the green gloom.
   This moor, wrinkled and fathomless:
our elder, our beloved, our wasteful past,
our elemental birth and nurture,
   Wait, wait for us in the slow adagio
of your history.
   O love, let us be true to one another:
the wild dark and the bright day!

Morning Prayer

HELP ME I murmur
as if I knew
to whom I speak
or what I'm asking for.
　　Sitting in my nightgown
for coffee by the window,
walking up Third Avenue,
waiting in my studio by the clay bins,
　　O help me,
and sometimes I hold my breasts
and a stronger pulse beats upwards
as if my words are both prayer and answer.
Help me —
as if somewhere a great ear listens
to our morning roar,
an orbit swings open
and the Spirit of Love like a sharp bite of acid
etches the ground and I can lift my foot.
　　Help me to feel your presence
in grain and grape,
not to wander as if lost
when I am not lost.
Sweeten my breath from the fantasy
I am not loved nor touched enough.
For ecstasy breathes at the window where I wait,
leaps toward me in little gasps
of the cock's trembling comb,
the hen's groan, the maple catkins
hanging like green teats, the dawn's pallor.
　　I am stroked by the darting dapple
Hopkins praised! Help me
to feel faithfully your presence
riding under the surface
in a mighty unwasted current.

All our Relations

Mother I

My mother was beautiful. Not glamorous—Beautiful! When I knew her, her figure was matronly, her ankles slim, her hair was silvery grey, and her brows darker like a gentle charcoal. Her complexion was peaches and cream — natural color in her cheeks, pink lips, a sweet smile and a musical laugh. I loved to watch her do her hair, especially when she put it up in a French roll. A French roll goes up the back of the head, vertical, very elegant, I thought. And there were always little curls that escaped on her neck, little vortices I could put my finger in. Just a touch, so intimate.

My mother was smarter and quicker than the rest of us (four children and a husband) and she was often sarcastic and demanding of more than we could do. But that was because we were "the jewels in her crown," as she would say — we were her Life. In the early mornings when I would come downstairs to eat breakfast and go to school, I would find her in the pantry, leaning into herself against the bins. I knew she had been crying because there were funny little red spots around her lips. When I was older, I asked her what was wrong. She said, mournfully, that she needed more tenderness. I think she meant from my father.

Oh how little we understood one another's hungers. Now I am seventy-eight. My mother has been dead for many years. I would try to do it all very differently now. When I was an adolescent, I didn't understand her frustration. "Do you love me?" she asked as we walked home together from the high school. Of course I loved her, I said, she was my mother. Like, I have no choice. "You are a devil!" she said. I didn't know what she meant.

My mother died when she was fifty-seven years old. I was twenty, just about to graduate from Reed College in Portland, Oregon. She didn't want to die. She had cancer of the left breast and refused surgery, preferring to follow a natural path of diet and carrot poultices — with a woman doctor who was sure this was the way. It took a year and a half. She died at home. We were all called to her bedside. She was propped up on pillows, like a queen on a throne. And she was exhorting us to behold the chariot and white horses coming for her. It was bizarre and unforgettable. "I forgive you, Jess," she said to my father. "I forgive you, too, Lily," he replied testily, as if he suspected he had been upstaged, and unfairly so.

The neighbors thought I should come home and stay with my mother to care for her. I didn't want to do that. She was being cared for and I wanted to continue my life at college. So I would ride my bike home frequently to visit her. There wasn't much to say, but one time she surprised me by turning her head toward me, looking into my eyes, and saying "It doesn't really matter whom you night with." I think she was referring to the fact that I had a boyfriend-lover at school, would be out all night, but there was always some other explanation. I was struck by her use of the word *night* as a verb. Something mythic about it. It was all very indirect and camouflaged, but I was deeply affected by the change in her, that enabled her to look at me that way. Letting go.

My sister and brothers all smoked cigarettes. My mother was terrified I would begin. She knelt on the floor on her two knees and begged me not to smoke. She pleaded. She wept. It didn't do any good. I would climb out of the window of the attic where I slept and climb onto the roof and light a cigarette and watch the smoke travel and dissolve. I was not a heavy smoker. When I was about fifty, my body rebelled and I had to stop. My lungs refused to breathe in the intoxicant.

My mother died in April, in the spring. We dressed her in the beautiful pink silk kimono with white cherry blossoms which I had brought her from Hawaii the summer before. I had gone as a traveling companion with another Reed student. My mother looked beautiful in pink even though she was not herself any more, but cold and lifeless. I touched her head. It was like a cold stone. I picked lilies of the valley from our garden and put a sprig in her hands. At the funeral, in a funeral home, the family all sat in a special room. My brother Ralph, twenty-four, came from Chicago where he was studying piano with Rudolf Ganz at the Chicago Musical College. He was extremely gifted, and he was the only blue-eyed child in our family and very handsome. I remember how he was shaken with sobs. I didn't know he could cry like that or that he cared for her so much.

When my mother was nine years old, her mother died in childbirth with the ninth child. Her father not knowing what else to do, gave the children away. The infant, Jerry, was no problem. But the others, especially three little girls Mary, Lily, and Anna, seven to ten years old, were not so easy "to get rid of." So, as my mother told the story: One morning the three sisters set out walking hand in hand down the country road in Indiana looking for a place to live. Soon they realized they would have to split up. My mother was given a try-out at a couple of places, but didn't stay. In one place she had to sleep with the dog, and didn't like that. Finally she was taken in by a Quaker family in Pendleton, Indiana, Neil and Laura Hardy. My mother was a capable and willing little girl and soon felt like one of the family. She and my father had a Quaker wedding.

Haunted by rejection, hungry for reassurance, insecure always in affection, my mother's destiny was inherited by her children. I and my sister, especially, have had to wrestle with these ghosts. I think I have made friends with them and tamed them to some degree. Hopefully, this will help my mother to greater freedom in the next go-round.

... from my poem "Alchemy":

> When my mother died,
> her mouth fell open.
>
> Five years later my father
> dropped ashes in the Columbia River
> from a bridge
> called The Bridge of the Gods.

165

Now I in alchemy
Here feel her shock,
His turning wrist intolerably,
Their letting go.

Now I may claim the gold from clay:
Years ago today I looked
And limped away; in my breast's alembic
Cupped the foolish face.

There cinders swung
Hot in the current of my grief,
Mixed with his fingers' slow relief.
Agitation rocked its vessel, clung.

Say imagination is my crucible:
Say in this tender, deeply torn,
The elements exchange occasion
For a sense; their last expenditure.

This miracle of change we seek
The chemistry of meaning we employ;
We reach for mystery and touch the heart,
Converted with the pain, our joy.

All our Relations

Father I

My father liked to eat rutabagas,
mashed, with butter. He liked
watermelon with a sprinkling of salt.
Dayold doughnuts, dayold bread.
My father could sing O dem golden slippers
in a sweet tenor voice.
After school and on Sundays
he would play ball with me in the street,
hitting grounders and flies
for me to chase and catch. He
took me to the barber and
got me a "boyish bob." I was 12.
When I wore scout knickers
you couldn't tell if I was a she or a he.
Boys would try to feel in my crotch
to see if I was lying.
   After college, after my mother died,
my father warned me about
the deep lines around my mouth:
parentheses from nostrils to chin.
Drama, he said. Your mother had them.
Your mother would get riled about something
and work on him to get him riled and
then when he was, she would be in a different mood,
would have forgotten her anger
and there he would be, shaking and a fool.
   He said, "As you get old
you'll get more and more like your parents."
And there is one way I can feel myself
like him more and more,
he liked to sit quietly, not talk,
not read — sometimes rock — just sit.
Seemed crazy and boring to others

but I can feel the stillness
busy with listening and looking,
that's enough.
My father's intensity took another way:
gears in neutral.

I liked to watch him shave.
He used a single blade razor
which he sharpened on a leather strap
hanging in the kitchen. He
would shave in front of the mirror
over the kitchen sink. If I asked him
he would shave my armpits.
My mother would dress the chicken
for Sunday dinner in that sink
on Saturday night. I watched her.
It was wonderful, especially when
she came to the egg sack, all those eggs
of different sizes, some almost ready
to be laid, so alive in the hen's body.
My father loved stewed chicken and gravy
and dumplings. The gravy
was always kind of yellow.

When I asked my father a certain kind of question
which he couldn't answer without further thought,
he would say he needed to think about it,
and he would carry the question sometimes for
several days, chopping wood in the basement
or rocking, and then one day he would say
I've been thinking about what you asked me
and this is what I think about it, and
then he would share with me his reflections.
My father was thoughtful in that sense,
given to thought. He had studied the law
as a young man. But it was his temperament too.
I always liked it when he would say
he would have to think about something.

All our Relations
Father # 2

Vulnerability

One day our family was having a meal
around our table in the dining room.
My father was serving. I must have been
11 or 12. I said something sarcastic
about my father's style — he was stingy
and we all suffered from it. To my surprise
he responded with words I have never forgotten.
They changed the way I saw my father.
He said, "Apparently you don't think
I have any feelings." I was thunderstruck.
It was true. I wasn't aware of my father's feelings.
He was serious, quiet, unexpressive, for the most part.
But now I was stung. I felt his hurt,
and I felt my own thoughtlessness,
shallowness, arrogance, selfishness.
I was embarrassed and ashamed.
It was an experience of revelation.
For you see it not only helped me to see my father
but it also alerted me to the feelings of others
who were perhaps unexpressive — or not easily
expressive of their tenderer feelings.
Many people are misunderstood, by themselves
as well as by those who are close to them.
Through the years, I have come to know
how important it is to speak to that vulnerability,
to be aware of it, to help it to speak.

All our Relations
The Gulf War

When the Gulf War came, I was paralyzed with horror and grief. I could not believe it was happening. I could not accept the hate and violence and waste. What could I do to help in this crisis? I felt impotent and bewildered. I could not let go of the images of destruction and suffering, nor could I make any move. I lay in bed in the middle of the night, unable to sleep, unable to get past the horror and confusion. Blocked, and locked in pain.

Suddenly a voice in my inner ear spoke to me. "This is not your war. This is not your human story. There are many stories to tell, and war is one of them, but it is not yours. You have other stories to tell, stories that human beings need to hear. You have not spent your life preparing to make wars. You and others must tell the stories you are stewards of. They will lead you through this barrier and this grief. You will be able to move again."

And I did begin to move, to breathe. The weight lifted from my breast. I could smile. I could hope. I could try to remember what stories I wanted to tell.

This is one of them: We should try to remember the stories we are stewards of, and tell them in whatever ways we can. We should try not to be overcome by forces which are alien to our souls. We do not need to fight. We need to sing, to sing out, to speak from an innocent place, a place of freedom. A place of vision in our souls. Let our true stories be part of world history.

All our Relations

God

I have had a big thought. It has moved my perspective right across the board to a radical change. It goes something like this:

To introduce it, I need to say that I sometimes describe myself as "disobedient." Actually what I mean is that OBEDIENCE is not one of my priorities. It all depends on what I'm asked to do. And even if I comply, I do so not out of obedience but out of agreement or imagination.

I am therefore sensitive to "mental sets" which assume power over others—which assume greater value, wisdom, importance. I am a religious person in that I have a strong sense of interconnection—a strong attraction to participation—a strong sense of joy and gratitude at the same time a sensitivity to pain and suffering and injustice. The word "religion" comes from the Latin and means to reconnect—To bind together again. It means an integration of our being and its many levels.

I do not often go to church services, and I have a problem with religious language which gives me a God whom we are to love, honor, and OBEY. Someone asked me recently, "What Master do you serve?" And I answered without hesitation, "I don't serve any Master," and I could feel myself bristle. I was surprised by the speed and energy of my response. For the idea of service (poetically understood) has always inspired me. Our lives are a service—they are a religious service. We touch each other when we can and give our gifts. It is a subtle matter to keep "service" free of reward—to keep it "gift."

In meditating on the question of control over and power over, I realized that the cultural language we inherit supports this pattern, We speak of the higher Self and the lower self; higher worlds; hierarchies—all terms which make legitimate a discrimination in favor of higher and against lower. This mental set is expressed also in the language of society: upper classes and lower classes, with the attendant prejudices. Religious scriptures stress that new life comes from the poor, the weak, the disabled, the meek.

The picture of God as a kind of parent-function does not work for me any more. And yet I struggle to find new ground (or let myself float free).

So, the Big Thought: Jesus said, "I and my father are one" and "Before Abraham was, I am." When I and my "father" are One, there is no "serving," there is union. I like this better. Is that what Love is, to feel the "union"—the mystical Oneness? before the beginning? We live in the Source, and the Source lives in us. It is a kind of transparency.

When I and my father are one, the dynamics of Obedience can be transformed into Mutuality and Integration.

Just a thought!

7 Musical Etudes on the Theme of Hope

This poem has had a long gestation.
Many years ago I woke from sleep with a sentence on my lips:
"Hope is the rhythm of loving without ejaculation."
A shocking sentence, as dream sentences often are.
I have carried this sentence as a kind of meditation, until
it birthed this poem. The sentence and the poem tell us
that Hope is not end-gaining. Hope is always becoming,
always expectant. Hope does not die into satisfaction,
but lifts always, anticipates, listens to what comes next.
The poem may be read in this way: each word or phrase
sounding and then listening to the next.

I

HOPE
and as is, is
lacking beforehand without
within wanting and afterwards
sky solemn seamstress awfully whether
yet
the wish waiting circumstance
loftily underbelly wanting but not ever
the landing
the HOPE bone and interim, will be,
and the answering

OH HOPE
and is is whereabouts
awe meander and
HOPE

> HOPE sky
ground altar otherwise
Oh and Oh if
but where uncanny uncouth yes
HOPE IS AS BY BUT WITH AND
tendency, wish
and whereabouts
> HOPE and if what went
OH yes again you HOPE
grace ploughed that's it grace plumbed,
> OH HOPE sweet and a face,
marble, contour, and jeopardy —
passageway, lattice, peril   HOPE
> OH
> > wish particle and bridge

II

> HOPE

Oh HOPE imagine!
Bones and gong, the resonance,
OH Hope your sweet freedom
like scent nameless Oh Lark too bright, not
rapture, but HOPE, adrift, at home, the escalator
and we step off, no why, only the free and tender
absence.

BUT IS THERE ANY HOPE?

Everywhere.
Sand, slips through our fingers,
only HOPE, always
groundswell ebbtide doldrum

174

HOPE
        dissolves into presence,
images and stones, HOPE the flood the massacres
cruel hunger deep shadow blocking, HOPE weeps,
sees through. The sense of HOPE, itself, does not
discolor, underlies, overlays, an air, wound,
sound, universe breath in the inner ear.
      Love and vessel, remember,
reweave, receive, rhythmic,
beloved, be beloved, marry OH
                  HOPE
          and is is without

III

HOPE
        lap
            cradle
                spire
                    shell
visitor, veil and post
yet is not as yet is
oh laugh
        the care
              the cost
the evidence   the media
the transcript   justice and mercy
truth openhanded openhearted
waits, spinning, the weft
OH HOPE   yet is is
before and after — the Lazarus leap,
the tooth fairy, wait, HOPE,
recall — always the beginning,

canyons and walls, if you will,
or is any at least as

HOPE
   faithful to process
the coiling cradling burying
badgers bailiffs oh touch,
the sense of touch who can be
what shall I and do —
prospects the heavenly host
cancellations postponements
HOPE, AH OH originally
yet yes the blackberry shrivelling
uneaten unpicked unpainted
understood OH yes HOPE
understood
to be as is is

   open and feeling, gift,
riddles, plunge, soar
sensual destiny withdraw
withhold
   HOPE
     not
withdrawn withheld
HOPE sits its horse
  the horse sweaty and cool
maddened by moon,
  runs,
tacks, turns, retells
the tale — the HOPE:
star grub
snail's glisten exhalation
of dust — ready, ready

to   OH HOPE   imagine
as is is OFF

invisible the vine the reach
catapult crease   light in a wheat field
sun   set   meteors   sainthood
the clasp   OH HOPE
                              endangered
resurrects

                    IV

    Lift   lift
Cassius a lean look —
    incense   sage   smudge
will it, oh pure to be —
    Bainbridge Davis   83   went
for a hike, died on a hillside
smack   OUFF   like that
serving joy, slipped out of sight
and yet   the hollow
the cupped hands,   the sharp nose
on track   on the track   where
HOPE   if
                as is, is   can't
cut, can't say when — not
to know, can be
                    otherwise
How lovely it is here,
                    abandoned,
                    immune
        LOTUS

forming, the mud, what next.
    Love lifts us to look over,
to see if   yet   what   but the wall
the secret finding a way,   HOPE unfolding

does not preside,   does not contain
is certain of what   HOPE ha

John Cage said
    nonsense
nonsense is
nonsense is the language of lovers,
the language lovers talk to each other in.
What are we saying when
we talk HOPE?

V

HOPE   IS
THE   RHYTHM   OF   LOVING   WITHOUT   CLIMAX
without goal,   rhythm sustained,
loving sustained, no ending, no release,
listening become an organ not an activity,
new organs of perception, new organs of love
not part of reproduction — a sexuality of the body
not the genitals,   desire in the fingers
to caress   the skin   expressing tenderness,
not invasive,   not suffocating, —
not to possess or be possessed
but to touch and be touched, free to be loved,
no consequences, no responsibilities, no cost,
a free gift — shall we give each other HOPE,
a free gift: no babies, no rape, no frigidity,

178

no fear, no shame, no guilt, no past

　　　　　　　　— OH HOPE

when I do　then I can tell your stories
gratitude and mystery and praise and humor
stories of love sustained　broken　as　we　are
its　rhythms　heal our uncertainty　oh HOPE
stewards of horror and grief become storytellers
of lifemagic: this tiny voluptuous rounded seed
like enameled gold from a locust pod, tiny, finished
in detail, what for　for the rhythm of life　for fun
for waste　for heaven　for seedpower in the etheric realm,
for elegance of HOPE, no guarantee, but HOPE.
Eliot said it would be hope for the wrong thing, maybe so,
if we hope for a purpose.　NO　NO
to hope is to forswear
purpose
to keep faith, with the reins loose on the horse's neck,
a gentle mouth

　　　So much pain and disappointment, so much frustration,
how hope?　How not?
We start at a new point and proceed to
a different kind of journeying —
yes, starting over, learning
to wait　wait to digest and excrete　wait to hunger anew:
the new innocence　the new intimacy
Here they are:　the new parents:　innocence and intimacy,
busy with daytoday process, daytoday HOPE, daytoday LOVING

It is a music.
It lives in the beat, the caesura, the rest.
HOPE is a music whose rhythms
are not resolved, are expectant, ready
to respond with the next progression —

And yet and yet

to be without HOPE is
to make demands, assumptions, expectations —

OH HOPE   you disarm

VI

OH HOPE
              is not the whole thing.
Hope is if you want it /
want HOPE   give up the rest
let go the known
   kiss the fleeting dream
kiss her feet   can you   can you   is it
is it   possible   to HAVE HOPE —
to have what you hope for —
is there a time when HOPE
changes into image, births, then,
   HOPE the solace of fantasy
an imagined desire

HOPE, you suddenly bloom blue
on the fence, singing la   la   la   la

The plums rot before they are ripe.

The pollen does not reach the grain —
   the silk channel of desire
      for seed
        for progeny

OH HOPE
    an aureole around the plantain's crown,
    the ugly white fungus on the cob
organisms toward birth   are   we
do   we
            OH HOPE   do   we   always   have   to
compelled by our long history?
Can we spring blue in the void
    speak love in the abyss
can we hear the unheard-of
    lacquer
the gloss   the shine   the glory
of goodness?
    can we
HOPE
       can we hear the news
can we go, stay, be present,
  belong?

I am stirred always by the beauty
  of the body
               beautiful — thigh   upper arm
soft hair   beard   bosom   barefoot,
the beautiful face, the laugh, the sigh,
the sob, the yawn, the belch, the shout —
    the one who is here shines so
a veiled presence to the senses in
    imagination

skin old and cold like cathedral steps sublime

"I don't count," Bernard said, thinking of the beauty of his wife,
"I'm holding my own," he said.

And passion   the passion we live by   the lust
   the lying in wait, oh   those   sweet   thrusts
   and   invitations
                  yes we do
toward seed
         the lover imagined in replica

yet

Oh HOPE
        defy the bullying of history
Breathe
       and
          Smile
from the Muse
         her amusement
               music
indescribable: FACE TO FACE

Oh the body of HOPE — the throat
   forming an embryo
          a HOPE
Here the Halleluia
   give up all you have

the quickening ear

              VII

word-
    ness
utter-
    ance

the single sound   as is, is
Tom   Eleanor   Daisy Tim   Rose
   OH HOPE   genuinely
await,
               pleasure   as is   soul
this interval
           this tempo and pitch
this duration   sustainable
OH seismic interval
   galaxies
        the original note

words
       birth in the ear,
  beings born
Huh   ha   rid   rid of
  call   call out   speak
intone   evoke HOPE'S realm   in tongues

to be a word, spoken by another   AH   LOVE
is it
   named   called
to not know   to answer
AH   THIS   DANCE on air is,
                        on breath
soundless
   THIS   WORD   gesture of body
larynx   womb
              one note
one at a time
one   instant   all   as is, is
and each   the cosmos   the web
     each   is

The Beginning of My 80th Calendar Year:

I meant to go straight home
but the rose garden called me.
I picked a yellow bud splashed with orange,
I picked a camellia, and a deep purple bloom.
I put water in my coca cola glass
    and made a bouquet —
so elegant, so full, so natural.

I had been throwing cups on the potter's wheel,
    the torn ones let the light through.

What shall I do to celebrate my 80th year?
    my 80 years?

O gladsome, O sadsome, O jingle O jangle,
the air grows thin as we get to the top —
O wingsong a thingsong,
heaven's kettle is humming.
    Drink me, O time to come,
    swallow me whole and tell the thirsty sparrows
    how I was translated!

I hope there's music up ahead,
of course there is,
where else would it come from —

All my years I have spent
    coming toward music,
    emergent to music,
baffled, blinded, immersed
in this intrinsic ballad,

this aubade, this fandango,
this chorale — this air!

Why am I running ahead, to hear the first notes?

The first 75 years were the hardest:
so much to unload, unlearn, undo —
so much sweetness to receive,
so much grief to let go.

I put the flowers in the gap
between the sliding windows
to catch the sunset light —
the last light of 1995 —
The sky is aflame with its passionate adieu,
its passionate leavetaking.

FAREWELL FAREWELL TOMORROW IS ANOTHER YEAR!

All these numbers and concepts and *things*
we call culture seem ephemeral to me.
They are passing away.
Our bodies are passing away.
History unmasks the vanishing river.

That moment on the beach when all the bright stuff
vanished into light
and I said, "Behold!"
The change from wave to spray to distance:
Behold! Something not visible
    or nameable
           translates the energy of time
and age and person
into REVELATION.

We are sounds in an unheard-of music.

Closing Birthday Prayer
(July 13, 1996)

But

can I   will it   are you   whenever   anywhere

your head in this wet clover,
your body in the hammock of these cornflowers

     O justice   O compassion

Plead   Plead   for us

in a murderous time (a poet writes)
the heart breaks and breaks
and lives by breaking

I want to tell you — I want you to know

    how important we are to each other,

how we create the world for each other

    and more,

how the bright riff of sunlight

    burns with our lust

    our warmth

Oh baby   hold me — hold this
    laughter and caring,
this awful pain of letting go,
this abyss of flaring life,

make new

make death a parade, outa sight,

disappearing
reappearing from the opposite direction
in the costumes of rising planets,

Singing this day this hour this place these people

and...

    can you

    will we

    is it?

Give me the message, baby, give me the good news.

Can I call you mom?

Can I call the world friend and beloved,

is it okay to be in love looking out through perforations of starlight?

It's cosmic all right,

its's *so* cosmic —

    the courage to press on,

to feed our hunger, to play with our child,

to bake bread, clean house, drive, sleep, eat,

    suffer,

(*sous* faire) — to *under*go

    to suffer our experiences.

can I   will we   do you

    and the rain, can it?

the trees and earth   the heavenly hosts

the singing of angels

the devil's play?

It's a mouthful — this prayer
   of birthday gratitude
for village, for friends, for the mystery
            of now

Biographical Sketch

by Deborah J. Haynes

The work of Mary Caroline Richards is known within diverse communities: to many, she needs no introduction. M. C. has taught at both traditional and alternative educational institutions. As the author of *Centering* (1964, reprinted as a twenty-five year anniversary edition in 1989), *The Crossing Point* (1973), *Toward Wholeness: Rudolf Steiner Education in America* (1980), and *Imagine Inventing Yellow: New and Selected Poems* (1991), she is widely read and much appreciated. *Centering* established M. C.'s public voice; *Crossing Point* gathered talks and essays from 1964–1971. The essays, poems, and paintings in the present volume, covering 1980–1996, bring M. C.'s published works up to the present.

Her work has historical significance: she was a participant in the famous educational experiment, Black Mountain College; and her work in the visual arts has for many years challenged dominant distinctions between art and craft. The fact that her pots are in many major and private collections in the world testifies to their perceived importance.

Although M. C. narrates her own story in "Toward M. C." and provides a detailed account of her experiences at Black Mountain College in her talk included here, a brief biographical sketch at this point will help to place her in time and space. Her life demonstrates a unique blending of the spiritual and artistic, and her published work may be read as an extended philosophy of creativity.

Mary Caroline Richards was born in Weiser, Idaho in 1916. Early in her life, her family moved to Portland, Oregon. She was the youngest of four, with two brothers and one sister. The gift of a book of poems, translated by Arthur Waley, during her community college years at Saint Helen's Hall, stimulated an interest in Oriental poetry and an aspiration to become a sinologist. At Reed College, although there was no formal Oriental Studies department, she was able to write a bachelor's thesis on T'ang poetry in relation to western imagism. M. C. followed this keen interest in Oriental culture, language, and mysticism by undertaking graduate work at the University of California in Berkeley. While there, however, her focus changed to English and linguistics: her doctoral dissertation was on irony in the writing of Thomas Hardy.

Two aspects of her early training seem significant in relation to the development of M. C.'s unique worldview and path. First, her study of Chinese ideograms gave her an appreciation for the links between writing and drawing, what she calls "writing as handcraft" or "writing-as-drawing." Even the essays and talks collected in this volume reflect this orientation to writing as an embodied and visual practice. Second, her involvement with Hardy's work engaged her in larger questions about the nature of appearance and reality. Both of these themes would resonate repeatedly in M. C.'s life, as she later became familiar with Zen Buddhism, then with the ideas of Rudolf Steiner, and as her own worldview evolved.

After graduate school, M. C. had a succession of jobs, in Washington state, New Mexico, and at the University of Chicago. In the 1940s she and her husband, Albert William Levi, had an opportunity to go to Black Mountain College, where they became involved in community and experimental education. During this early period at Black Mountain, Robert Turner introduced her to clay, which became a central metaphor and practice in her life. Significant intellectual and personal relationships were also initiated during these years, with the ideas of Rudolf Steiner and Carl Jung, with avant-garde musicians John Cage and David Tudor, and with dancer Merce Cunningham, among others.

M. C. had first heard of Rudolf Steiner in 1949, when she was in London looking for a school for her nine-year-old stepdaughter. A brochure from the Ministry of Education, which described Steiner's approach to growth and learning, piqued her curiosity. A few years later, David Tudor gave her Steiner's books on education and she met Francis Edmunds, a Steiner teacher from England, at Spring Valley, New York. Steiner's vision of community formation was especially vivid for her. Still later, in the early 1960s when the Camphill movement was brought to the United States, M. C. responded to the imaginative vision of the Camphill schools and villages, communities for developmentally disabled adults based on Steiner's ideas. Her book, *Toward Wholeness*, describes her journey in relation to Steiner's philosophy, Anthroposophy, and it also discusses Waldorf (Steiner) education in America.

After leaving Black Mountain with Tudor in 1951 (it "adjourned" a few years later), they lived in New York City for three years, then decided to organize another community with people who had participated in the College. As M. C. puts it, they were "supposed to go rather light on the community aspect." On 110 acres near Stony Point, New York, she set up a pottery studio with Karen Karnes and David Weinrib, where she lived with Tudor and worked until 1964.

In 1961 she was recommended by Francis Merritt to speak at a regional meeting of Connecticut craftpersons at Wesleyan University. Her subject was "Centering as Dialogue." As a result of that lecture, she was invited by Wesleyan University Press to expand its themes into a book for their new Interdisciplinary Studies series. *Centering* was the result of that effort, and was well received. M. C. subsequently lived alone in New York City while teaching at City College. She also traveled to England in 1966, and there studied projective geometry with Olive Whicher at Emerson College, which later would be one of the inspirations for her second book, *The Crossing Point*, published in 1973. While in England, serendipitous meetings with Seonaid Robertson and Charity James, both of whom taught at Goldsmith College, University of London, led to a visiting position in the curriculum laboratory of the college. These experiences were especially formative for M. C.'s understanding of collaborative learning.

When she returned to the United States, M. C. began to lead clay workshops in North Carolina at Penland School of Crafts, in Maine at Haystack, and in Pennsylvania, where she was then sharing a studio with artist Paulus Berensohn on his farm near Uniondale, Pennsylvania. For many years she worked intermittently in Camphill villages; then, in 1984 she moved to one of the Camphill centers as a coworker. She continues to travel, lecture, and teach.

It is very difficult to summarize M. C.'s life, her worldview, or her work in the world, for she has clearly followed her own intellectual and spiritual path. The evocative power of her life story and of her essays and talks, her poetry, and art must be directly experienced by the reader and viewer.

Afterword

by Deborah J. Haynes

Here, at the end of *Opening Our Moral Eye*, I want to engage in a brief dialogue with M. C. Richards' new essays, thereby demonstrating something of their scholarly and personal vitality. But before entering into a formal dialogue, a few comments about the nature of dialogue itself are in order. This, of course, is very much in keeping with M. C.'s own process of writing and teaching. Linguistics, clarity of definition, to reflect about where we are headed while we are on the journey!

My conception of dialogue has been formulated through reading and thinking about the ideas of the Russian moral philosopher Mikhail Bakhtin. Dialogue, for Bakhtin, is a timeless and ultimately unfinalizable process. Works of art, literary or visual, can break through the boundaries that demarcate past and present. "Great works," in his view, can live intense and fuller lives in the present than they did during their own time. Of course, the question of what constitutes a great work is highly ideological and subjective; my goal here is not to assert or promote the relative greatness of M. C. Richards's writing. I do hope, however, that a dialogue with the essays in this book will demonstrate their relevance and vitality.

In his last published essay of 1974, Bakhtin reaffirmed the timeless quality of dialogue. "There is neither a first nor a last word and there are no limits to the dialogic context (it extends into the boundless past and the boundless future). Even past meanings, that is, those born in the dialogue of past centuries, can never be stable (finalized, ended once and for all)—they will always change (be renewed) in the process of subsequent, future development of the dialogue...."[1]

In other words, thinking itself is a dialogical process: There is no such thing as individual thought. We hold imaginary dialogues with others; we internalize their voices, their values. There are no limits to dialogue. The surprising and unpredictable quality of this process is evident not only in our interactions with others, but internally, within the self as well. New meanings are born; old meanings change. M. C. has functioned for me as such a dialogic Other. My inner dialogue, as well as the actual dialogue with her over a number of years, has helped me not only to articulate what I think but also to form the self I have become and am becoming. Dialogue does not end, unless we cut it off.

In the first two essays of *Opening Our Moral Eye,* M. C. provides details of her biography. "Toward M. C." was the result of a series of conversations in 1985 with Gerry Williams, editor of *Studio Potter* magazine. "Black Mountain College: A Personal View of Creativity" was given as a talk in 1992, during a celebration of this educational experiment. Here she discusses many of her formative influences: her parents, educational experiences at Reed College, the University of California, and Black Mountain; her early work translating Antonin Artaud; people such as Robert Turner, John Cage, David Tudor, Olive Whicher, Charity James, Seonaid Robertson, and Paulus Berensohn; particular clay series,

---

1. Published in Mikhail M. Bakhtin, *Speech Genres and Other Late Essays,* trans. Vern W. McGee, ed. Caryl Emerson and Michael Holquist (Austin: University of Texas Press, 1986), p. 170. My own understanding of dialogue has been enriched by studying Bakhtin and other philosophers such as Martin Buber. But I am also indebted to two of the finest interpreters of Bakhtin's ideas: Caryl Emerson and Gary Saul Morson. See especially their *Mikhail Bakhtin: Creation of a Prosaics* (Stanford: Stanford University Press, 1990) and my *Bakhtin and the Visual Arts* (New York: Cambridge University Press, 1995).

such as the seven "I Am's"; her experience with Waldorf education, Rudolf Steiner's ideas, and the decision to live in a Camphill
Village community. Many themes surface in this narrative of her
own life story, but three of them stand out in my reading: the role
of irony, Artaud's idea of "virtual efficacy," and M. C.'s ambigu-
ous relationship with academia.

Irony means using words or an image to express a contradictory
meaning, a meaning that is the opposite of what is usually
intended. While irony shares with sarcasm and satire a sense of
mockery, irony alone exploits the paradoxes or contradictions of
events, things, or persons. As M. C. puts it, irony occurs when you
say one thing but mean another. To point out the disjunction
between reality and appearance can be an act of cultural criticism.
In the contemporary arts, irony has too often lost its place to various forms of parody and pastiche. Irony requires a high degree of
subtlety and intellectual sensitivity, while parody and pastiche are
more heavy-handed.

Certainly, parody has positive uses: Here I am thinking of Linda
Hutcheon's description of parody's *para* as not only counter or
against, but also near and beside.[2] In this sense, parody may
involve entering into genuine dialogue with work of the past; and
it may carry ironic overtones. Pastiche, the random cannibaliza-
tion of aesthetic styles of the past from a kind of shopping mall of
history, is less benign. I see much parody and a distressing amount
of pastiche in the arts today; I wish I saw more irony. M. C.'s essays
express at times a refreshing ironic sensibility.

In our world of virtual realities and virtual worlds, Artaud's idea
of "virtual efficacy" seem prescient. While translating Artaud' s *The
Theater and Its Double,* M. C. was especially impressed by his
understanding of the theater as a potential place for personal and
cultural transformation. Neither thinking nor acting were literal in

---

2. Linda Hutcheon, "Theorizing the Postmodern," in *The Post-Modern Reader,* ed.
Charles Jencks (London: Academy Editions, 1992), p. 87.

this "alchemical theater"; both only appeared to be efficacious. But the "virtual" nature of this setting could also enable "actual" change.

Have we totally lost this sense of possibility? In a world of neo-noir "kool killer" movies such as *Natural Born Killers, The Last Seduction,* and *Pulp Fiction* and violent computer games, where is the line between screen fiction and real-life fact? I fear this line may be blurred for whole generations of young people. "Virtual efficacy" may be left to the imaginations of older citizens, while youngsters and adolescents play in virtual reality. Actual social transformation and social renewal, so much a part of M. C.'s utopian vision, may become less and less possible unless they are consciously affirmed.

M. C. has had an equivocal relationship with academia, what Mary Daly frequently calls "academentia." Educated at fine institutions (Reed College and the University of California, Berkeley), she had several teaching positions during the 1940s, 50s, and 60s before becoming a free-lance teacher. For many years now M. C. has had no official position in a university or college, and has in fact been critical of the processes of socialization and the lack of true education that too frequently characterize educational institutions.

Educators and activists such as Paolo Friere advocate learning to question as a pedagogical tool for developing linguistic, social, and political consciousness. Ivan Illich had written that schools teach students the need to be taught, which prepares them for the alienation and institutionalization of life that awaits once schooling has been completed. Students are "schooled" to confuse teaching with learning, grade advancement with education, a diploma with competence, fluency with the ability to say something. By inculcating the idea that there is only one main authority and one right answer (the teacher's), schools thus destroy the desire to learn. This is a devastating critique of public school education. Long before I knew Friere's or Illich's ideas, I had already learned—in my first ceramics courses with David Stannard—that following the meandering way of questioning led me not necessarily on the quickest route from here to there, but on an authentic quest. Like Stannard, M. C. did not articulate her criticism of the educational system directly, but she practiced another pedagogy.

Although she long ago eschewed a full-time position, M. C. has had many opportunities to work in various academic settings: art departments in large state universities, private colleges, and institutions devoted to Waldorf education and training teachers in Steiner's method. In recent years, she has worked with Matthew Fox in the Institute of Creation Spirituality at Holy Names College. To all of these settings she brings her commitment to fostering the development of the person through cross-disciplinary creativity workshops. If M. C. has remained a maverick in academic settings, the fact that so many universities and colleges over the years have provided her with opportunities to teach confirms that they remain the primary patron of the arts. Even so, within the academy the arts are often considered marginal to a liberal education.

In many ways Black Mountain College was an ideal, if ultimately transitional, educational environment, for it combined three significant elements: community life, intellectual study, and artistic experience in the studio. For M. C. those three elements are central to her ongoing life at Camphill Village.

M. C.'s ideas about education are articulated in "The Public School and the Education of the Whole Person," originally published as a booklet by Pilgrim Press in 1980. When she wrote this essay, public education was already in crisis; that crisis has not abated in the subsequent years. In fact, the crises may be even more extreme. The ongoing challenges of cultural pluralism, including the basic problem of language when students are increasingly diverse, of the impact of new technologies, including the computer and television, and of the neglect of the inner life of the teacher all result in a complex situation that demands innovative responses.

Teachers, M. C. suggests, should stay with their students over a period of years, fostering respect for the individual gifts of each child. Moral imagination should be cultivated alongside cognitive knowledge. "The creative power of the individual hand" should be fostered through all of the arts, while the individual disciplines themselves should be infused with the broader disciplines of will, sincerity, and wholeness. Education should be understood as a lifelong process, not confined to a few years in elementary and high schools, but extending throughout the span of life. Nevertheless, the public school has a significant double role: to provide continuity in the transmission of culture and to stimulate the courage for change and transformation. A profound idealism that is still much needed pervades M. C.'s vision of humanity.

Perhaps the most striking feature of the 1992 talk, "After Wholeness, What?" is its articulation of the role of outrage in both personal development and social-political engagement. Here, as elsewhere in her writing, M. C. uses her own experience to pose significant questions. On the one hand, working to attain wholeness involves training the self not to respond in anger to events and people around us, to develop what Buddhists would call compassionate acceptance. On the other, the actual process of becoming outraged at something or someone can be radicalizing in a positive way. What threshold do we cross? What outrages us? What prompts action? How long must we wait, passively observing, learning from what transpires around us, before we are moved to act? M. C. has seldom worked overtly on political causes, but rather she encourages the cultivation of a strong, and centered, inner self that can move confidently into the public sphere.

Of all the essays gathered here, "Imagination and Authenticity as Doorways to Creation" raises the most questions for me and provokes the strongest response. In this essay, M. C. affirms several ideas about the nature and development of the self. She speaks of an essential self and of the evolutionary development of consciousness and the spirit, ideas that are also articulated by Carl Jung (and Jungians such as Erich Neumann), and by Pierre Teilhard de Chardin and Sri Aurobindo. Like these writers, she believes that there exists both an individual and a collective consciousness, a kind of creative unconscious. Like Rudolf Steiner, she affirms the existence of an inner self that is free of cultural programming, suggesting that knowledge is possible free of the gendered body.

This is not the place to rehearse arguments about essentialism that continue to rage in both academic and popular literature. From Alison Jaggar and George Lindbeck to Camille Paglia, writers argue about whether human beings are constituted by essential biological categories or whether language and culture are determinative in establishing gender and other aspects of the self.

My own relationship to these ideas has evolved significantly during the last two decades. From an early sympathy with Jung's ideas, for instance, I have developed greater affinity with the cultural-linguistic model, which emphasizes the way consciousness and the self differ depending upon the cultural context. I no longer confidently believe in a collective consciousness, nor in a self that exists free of cultural programming.

But my reaction to this essay is not just one of query or disagreement. In "Imagination and Authenticity" M. C. also discusses the imagination as the sense organ that perceives spirit in matter. Imagination is a concept with a long and vivid history. The word is derived from the Greek and Latin words, *phantasia, eikasia,* and *imaginatio*—fantasy, illusion, and imagination, respectively. It refers to the image-making capacity in human beings, which can be as varied as dreams, fantasies, illusions during daily life, artistic creativity, mystical visions, the ability to envision other people's lives or a better world. The vocabulary of imagination is slippery, and therefore it might be considered as more a myth than a concept. Like a myth, it has a complex history full of diverse interpretations.

I believe that imaginative activity must be placed in relation to and gauged by experience in the world. Analogously, as Wendell Berry once put it, the truth of the world's lives and places must be proved in imagination. Imagination for its own sake has a role in individual lives, as daydreams, fantasies, and reveries, but the greater work of imagination proceeds in relation to experience in the world. Imagination is not the special domain of the artist, but a capacity shared by all human beings. I agree with M. C., and with a host of other writers going back to Plato and Aristotle, that imagination is a faculty through which we experience the activity of the spirit in the world. Although she might not articulate it this way, I think that artists are under a strong injunction to develop and use this imaginative capability to its fullest creative and visionary potential.

M. C.'s writing is full of dynamic oppositions, two of which are compelling. First, she describes the tension between our failures—so vividly felt in the toxicity of our present environment—and the rediscovery of life sources and the sacred. Second, she identifies the tension between our practical and visionary capacities. We need to recognize our failures alongside a sense of the possibility of renewal of the sacred in the world; and we need to develop and hold both practical and visionary capacities in order to be whole human beings.

In "The Renewal of Art through Agriculture," a talk given in 1993 about her experiences teaching a course on this topic, M. C. describes art and agriculture as twins. As a result of living in the Camphill Village near Kimberton, Pennsylvania, M. C. has become an active community member and practitioner of biodynamic agriculture, the principles of which were first defined by Rudolf Steiner. Both art and agriculture depend upon careful observation of living processes, and they develop the powers of the imagination. She reminds us that the world is starved and starving, metaphorically and actually. While agriculture nourishes the body, art nourishes the soul and the imagination. Observation and intuitive improvisation are developed in creative work and in farming. These two activities nurture each other; both are necessary.

Her 1994 talk, "Creativity and the Practice of Awe," grew out of her experience with students who lack a sense of awe, and was given as part of Matthew Fox's program in Creation Spirituality. M. C.'s essay describes an abiding sense of pantheism that also reminds me of Ralph Waldo Emerson's small book, *Nature.* For Emerson, perceiving the beauty of natural forms is a delight. Through this beauty one senses a higher power, and the intellect strives to give it an order. But beauty is also related to moral values; it never exists only for its own sake.

Theologians such as Rudolf Otto identify experiences of awe, of the sublime and numinous, with the *mysterium tremendum*, the all-powerful, awe-full, and wholly Other mystery that surrounds us. Awe, for M. C., is a practice, a way to measure our relationship to and connection with the cosmos. Awe is the ground for work with our sorrow and grief, and it is the ground for social justice work.

Opening Our Moral Eye also contains plates of M. C.'s recent paintings and a series of new poems titled "Before the Beginning." I do not want to, and really cannot, discuss her paintings or poetry in a discursive manner. But, I will end this reflective ending essay with a few remarks about them.

I first saw some of M. C.'s paintings in the summer of 1991 at Kimberton Hills. We unfurled them on the porch of the house, and we pinned one to the long wall in the pottery studio. Then, in May 1994, I saw her exhibition at Holy Names College. I sat alone for a long time in the room, looking and musing. These paintings do not reveal their power in a brief encounter. But if the viewer is willing to look, and *to see,* they carry visual power and offer keen visual pleasure.

When I first read the poems collected here, I was reminded of Giambattista Vico. Many of our linguistic metaphors are drawn from bodily and erotic life, as Vico already observed in his seventeenth-century book, *The New Science.* The head is the top or beginning. We speak of the shoulders of a hill, the eye of a needle, the lip of a cup, the teeth of a rake, the tongue of a shoe, the bowels of the earth, and so forth. Fields are thirsty, willows weep:

numerous other examples could be given. Vico's "vision" involved hands that are not afraid to touch the earth and yet remain capable of reaching out to embrace other persons.

I feel this same sensibility in M. C.'s writing. We have barely begun to understand the unique visionary powers of hearing and touch. Hearing is perhaps the most abstract of the senses, while through touch our fundamental relationship in and to the world is formed. From Feuerbach to feminist philosophy and theology, many writers have understood the formative role of touch in forging ethical relationships through I-Thou encounters. But vision is also related to touch. Artists, for instance, learn contour drawing by developing their sense of the connection between eye/hand and the surface of the object or person being drawn. Such meditative practices of vision will help to train the gaze not to grasp, master, and seek to dominate what comes into its purview. It will help to awaken the other physical and subtle organs of perception. M. C. clearly knows this.

Finally, on hope. Like much of her prose and poetry, M. C.'s "7 Musical Etudes on the Theme of Hope" are both personal and philosophical. I agree with her that hope is not "end-gaining," but is always in the process of becoming.

For me, faith and hope come from the fact that new persons and new beginnings are forever being born as others die. Hope emerges out of a perspective that apprehends the ongoing creativity of life in the universe. But hope is not confidence; it is surrounded by dangers and may well be the consciousness of fragility and contingency.

Facing the contingency of human life and love, hope is profoundly different from optimism. Optimism is based on the conviction that everything will turn out well in the end, all adversities overcome in a final harmony. By contrast, hope is difficult to describe, more mysterious; it is inextricably linked to despair. Despair is an attitude of capitulation and acceptance, while hope implies a relaxed form of nonacceptance. Hope never fully accepts what is as the finalized end, but expresses this nonacceptance in an attitude of relaxation and patience.

Even more significant, however, is the notion that hope implies a special relationship to and consciousness of time. Despair sees time as a prison, closed and finalized. Hope is visionary, not in the sense that it sees what will be, but it affirms the future *as if* it sees further possibilities. Hope thus pierces the veil of time. Gabriel Marcel spoke of hope as the memory of the future.[3]

Hope is a memory of the future. What a strange and seemingly irrational statement! Hope refuses to see time as closed but understands that time is a spiraling continuity. Hope does not claim anything or insist upon its rights to anything in particular. Hope waits. How do we make sense of its central paradox? Hope implies a powerful role for memory. For it is only with a powerful memory of what *was* that we might be called to imagine a different future than the one we seem to be living-ourselves-into.

Integral to the process of waiting and imagining is the willingness to take risks. Our desires to have and to possess—objects, experiences, particular attainments, even perhaps the desire to create certain kinds of art and artifacts and to present them in the world—stand in the way of hope. Hope, like love, is a gift; it cannot be bought.

But where does hope come from, and why do we hope? These are clearly difficult questions to answer. Hope is like other virtues: love, charity, goodness, patience. Like them, hope can be refused, or it can be cultivated. Perhaps we hope because we are thinking and feeling beings—in a word, human. In M. C.'s poems, hope is the tune, the melody that trills in the ear, the music that helps us to open our moral eyes.

---

3. Gabriel Marcel developed this idea in "Sketch of a Phenomenology and Metaphysic of Hope," in *Homo Viator,* trans. Emma Craufurd (Chicago: Henry Regnery, 1951).

MARY CAROLINE RICHARDS has simultaneously lived several influential lives as potter, teacher, essayist, poet, and painter. She is the author of *Centering; The Crossing Point: Selected Talks and Writings; Toward Wholeness: Rudolf Steiner Education in America; Imagine Inventing Yellow; Before the Beginning* and the translator of Antonin Artaud's *The Theater and Its Double.* She has a doctorate in English literature from the University of California at Berkeley, an honorary doctorate in humanities from King's College, Pennsylvania, and has been on the faculty of Black Mountain College, the University of California, the University of Chicago, and the City College of New York. Her home is in a Camphill Village community with disabled adults in Kimberton, Pennsylvania, where the biodynamic method of agriculture is practiced.

. . . .

For a catalog of other books available from Lindisfarne Press please contact

L I N D I S F A R N E   P R E S S
RR 4 Box 94 A-1 Hudson, NY 12534
TEL : 518-851-9155   FAX : 518-851-2047